Barefoc
Cyberspace

Adventures in search of techno-Utopia

by Becky Hogge
illustrated by Christopher Scally

First published in 2011
by Barefoot Publishing
56 High Street, Hinxton
Saffron Walden, Essex CB10 1QY

Edited by: Damien Morris
Typeset by: Felix Cohen

ISBN: 978-1-906110-50-5

Becky Hogge was born in a village just outside Brighton, UK, in 1979. After graduating from Cambridge University in 2001, she worked as a music journalist, copy-writer, waitress and secretary before eventually establishing her name as a technology journalist specialising in bringing the alternative side of computer culture to the attention of a political audience. She has written weekly columns for the *New Statesman* on and off since 2006, and her writing has also been published in *openDemocracy.net*, the *Guardian*, *Index on Censorship*, *Prospect* and *Dazed and Confused.*

In 2007, she jumped the fence and became a full-time trouble-maker, joining grassroots digital civil liberties campaigners the Open Rights Group. For two years, she lead the organisation into battle against electronic voting, online censorship and mass communications surveillance before passing on the campaign baton in 2009 and moving to rural East Anglia. *Barefoot into Cyberspace* is her first book.

Contents

"Mankind's sole salvation lies in everyone making everything his business."

Alexander Solzhenitsyn

Prologue

Prologue: Fierce Dancing

When I was sixteen, I read a book called *Fierce Dancing: Adventures in the Underground.* It was written by CJ Stone, a columnist for the Big Issue, and it was about the free party and road protest movement in Britain. Although I was a bit too young to have ever been to a proper free party, to join convoys of crusties on the way to an unsuspecting field in the heart of the British countryside and dance straight for twenty hours, I'd been to the odd local rave. Around Brighton, where I grew up, sound systems could set up in a forgotten pocket of the South Downs for a few brief hours before being disturbed by a police force now empowered by the Criminal Justice and Public Order Act of 1994 to shut us down. We had a lot of fun.

Fierce Dancing filled in the blanks, it told the stories of the alternative cultures – pagans, new age travellers, punks and dropouts – that had coalesced around this scene and contributed to its vibrancy. It told tales of women who gardened vegetable plots in no knickers, tepee valleys in the depths of Wales, and how to make poppy tea. It was, in that most adolescent sense, a revelation. And to an adolescent growing up in the consumerist nineties, seven years after the fall of the Berlin Wall and seventeen years into the rule of Margaret Thatcher's Conservative party where alternative ideas about how to live seemed only to exist to sell ice cream and health drinks, it was also an escape. I'd often wondered what had happened to all the hippies. My favourite film at that time was *Easy Rider*. The legacy of the counterculture was celebrated in books and on TV, but, outside of the odd rave, the world around me seemed to contain little of the freedom, the rebellion and the exuberance that the sixties had supposedly promised.

For Stone, I suspect *Fierce Dancing* was a kind of eulogy. I suspect, from the way he speaks about them, that he didn't expect the communities he was recording to survive much longer. The book itself is now out of print. I spoke to its publisher at a drinks party recently, who told me that it had sold around 25,000 copies. That figure is, apparently, "not bad for a zeitgeist book".

Barefoot into Cyberspace, the book you're about to read, is a zeitgeist book, too. At least, that's what I intended it to be. At the end of 2009 I set out to record for posterity characters that, since I left adolescence and Brighton behind, had played key roles in the digital counterculture I eventually settled in to and that I suspected was about to disappear. These characters weren't the "rip, mix, burn", iPad-wielding social media consultants and purveyors of gadget-prop so often associated with the web. They were hackers and geeks, command-line cowboys, info-terrorists and civil libertarians. They had seen in the rise of many-to-many communications technology an opportunity to free modern society from corrupt institutions, to develop new ways of organising away from the imperative of industrial capitalism, and to seize agency and power from the jaws of the consumerist beast.

For the time that I travelled with them, I believed these things, too. I believed in them enough to abandon my career as a journalist and run an organisation called the Open Rights Group (ORG) which, as well as fighting to protect basic civil liberties online, campaigns against any kind of regulation that could prejudice the liberating aspects of the 'net. I don't run ORG anymore, which is probably a good thing given how sceptical I became that its mission could succeed. It wasn't that I didn't think the techno-Utopians were onto something. I simply feared that the institutions of the old world they thought they could topple – be they corporations, media or politicians – had a lot of fight left in them.

But if *Barefoot into Cyberspace* was intended to be a eulogy, I hadn't figured on WikiLeaks. Almost from the moment I started collecting material for this book, their story began to trespass on mine. By the end of the year – 2010 – in which the majority of this book was written, the culture I'd been a part of for almost a decade was headline news all over the world. It's too early to tell what effect that will have on the techno-Utopian dream. All I can say is that it transformed this project from an exercise in cultural anthropology into something more like an adventure story. As a result, I had more fun writing this book than I could have imagined when I started it. I hope you enjoy reading it just as much.

Becky Hogge
June 2011

chapter
1
Digging the cmd Line

Chapter 1: Digging the command line

I may as well not have bothered. When I arrive, the event is already sold out. Stuck outside in the cold and slush, I'm hundreds of miles from home, wondering what on earth to do next. It's the day after Boxing Day, December 2009.

I'm not the only one to be disappointed. In front of me in the long queue by the entrance stands a young man from Bulgaria, who has travelled here alone and at great expense. He's speaking to one of the short, bearded volunteers marshalling the event, who has a badge pinned onto his chest saying "Here be Engels". It's only later I'll find out that he is not moonlighting as one of the founders of Communism, rather Engel is German for angel. Around him, crude signs flap in the breeze, sellotaped to the outer wall of the Berliner Congress Centre. Ink black marker etched onto A4 paper that is slowly disintegrating in the Berlin slush announces: "26c3 is sold out".

What's happening on the other side of the walls is the 26th annual congress of legendary German hacker collective the Chaos Computer Club. The organisation describes itself as "a galactic community of life forms, independent of age, sex, race or societal orientation, which strives across borders for freedom of information". The c3 of 26c3 translates as "c x 3" or "CCC", the acronym of both the event itself (the Chaos Communication Congress) and the organisation responsible for it. What's most frustrating is that CCC doesn't sell tickets in advance. The only thing any one of us could have done differently is fly out here earlier, and spend our Boxing Day queuing in a freezing cold Alexanderplatz instead of raising a glass with our families in the warmth back home.

Watching over us, across the snowy moonscape of eastern Berlin, is the Alexanderplatz television tower. A flying saucer spiked on a giant needle, it is the perfect vision of Soviet futurism. Twenty yards from the door at which it looks like my journey will end prematurely, a flock of municipal exhibition stands have come to rest on Alexanderplatz, commemorating the 20th anniversary of the fall of the Berlin Wall. Black and white photos of GDR rebels – crouched over printing presses pumping out samizdat, or else in small groups, smoking – look nonchalantly into the lens of posterity. Who took these photos? Which of their fellow freedom fighters knew we would want to look back on this congregation of young minds which changed the course of history? The photos are captioned in French, English and German, interspersed with grainy pictures of officials from the regime, the tortuous surveillance equipment of the Stasi, or the bright, art-punk graphics of the underground magazines that spread the rebels' message of freedom. The end of history stares flatly back at me through the glass as I breathe the steam rising from the cup of coffee I've bought from one of the Christmas market stands that fill the rest of the square.

I've come to 26c3 looking for new radicals, ones not yet preserved behind glass. The first Chaos Congress took place five years before the wall fell, when the ground I'm standing on still belonged to Frederick Engels. It was 1984, the venue was Hamburg, and if history was winding down, no-one had told the hackers yet. Wau Holland co-founded the Club three years earlier in 1981, in the offices of cooperative newspaper *Die Tageszeitung*. Legend has it that their inaugural meeting was held around a table salvaged from Kommune 1, a sixties experimental community linked to the violent darlings of the glamour-left, the "Baader-Meinhof" Red Army Faction. It was in Kommune 1 that the motto "the personal is political" (*Das Private ist politisch!*) was born.

Of course, that's pedigree, not politics, but the Chaos Computer Club showed their radical colours early on, too. In the year of the first Chaos congress, the club made worldwide headlines when members hacked the German Post Office's precursor to the internet, the expensive, private Bildschirmtext computer network. After bypassing the network's inadequate security measures, Chaos club members transferred DM134,000 from a major high street bank into the club's own account, returning the money the next day at a public press event at the bank's headquarters. Similar exploits followed, exposing the insecurity of systems in highly public ways and ostensibly for the public good, although fringe members of the group were also associated with more serious cases of cyber-espionage involving sorties into the networks of Los Alamos and NASA on behalf of the KGB. The Congress moved to Berlin in 1998, and has been held here annually ever since, nestling into the four days between Christmas and New Year, I suspect, because it keeps out the part-timers (like me), and makes it as cheap as possible to attend for those dedicated enough to fly out on Christmas Day.

Just like the reunified Germany, CCC commemorated its 20th birthday in Alexanderplatz. Its members chose a slightly more creative way to celebrate than the dull municipal billboards that are currently imprisoning these GDR radicals for a second time. *Blinkenlights*, derived from the hacker jargon for flashing computer screens, was a Space Invaders-style light show created in September 2001 on the side of the former Soviet HDL building just across the square. The CCC installed a set of computer-controlled lights behind the regular, square windows that covered the building to create a giant, pixelated screen, eight pixels high by 18 across, on which they played animations from dusk until dawn.

Over the years, the CCC has become a respected part of the German political landscape, its members frequently summoned to testify in front of legislators considering whether and how to regulate new technology. But it hasn't lost its radical side. In 2008, the club offered the fingerprints of the German Home Affairs minister – transferred onto a handy portable film – as a covermount to a popular hacker magazine, in order to demonstrate the fallibility and invasiveness of biometric identification systems. And by the sound of its latest hack, the CCC's radical spirit is alive, well, and tantalisingly close at hand.

Eventually, I get in. Journalists have their own ways of hacking access (we are hacks, after all), and I manage to convince the man at the ticket desk that it would be a bad move to exclude me. For the price of €80 – no press freebies here – I'm handed my press pass and told to wear it at all times. I am to be feared, approached tentatively. Nobody – and especially not the press – is permitted to document what goes on in parts of this conference, and I am on my honour to identify myself as a journalist to whomever I'm talking, in case they go on to incriminate themselves.

I'm here to interview Rop Gonggrijp, a Dutch hacker and activist, and a long-time friend of the CCC. And yes, I may have dropped his name at the desk to secure our entry, after all, at one time he was the Netherlands' most notorious hacker. But I'm sure he wouldn't mind. He's accustomed to the so-called "social hack". In 2006, Rop and his friends obtained decommissioned voting computers from a Dutch local authority in exchange for apple cake. He then proceeded to demonstrate on national television how the machines could be hacked to reveal and even alter what unsuspecting Dutch voters were keying in at the polling station. Unsurprisingly, the Dutch don't use electronic voting anymore in their elections, they vote with pencil and paper.

This is how I know Rop. When I was running the Open Rights Group we also campaigned to eliminate electronic voting from UK elections. But we didn't do any hacking. Instead, we sent security experts accredited by the UK's Electoral Commission to observe local and regional vote counts, filing our devastating report through the official channels. We were successful too. But I can't help feeling that the Dutch campaign was, well, just a hell of a lot cooler.

Inside the conference centre, it's all abuzz. Men and boys bustle in and out of the bar, which is dark, how they like it. The smell is of beer, grilled meat, and the outside brought in. The Berliner Congress Centre is laid out like a doughnut: wide, bright corridors encircle a central, domed atrium.

The feel is classic hack space – one part refugee camp, two parts Heath Robinson. All around the corridors conference furniture has been hijacked by the different European groups and clubs, many of whose members will be meeting each other "in meat space" for the first time. Shy boys with their heads plunged in laptops hide behind the distinctive liveries of local clubs which have been hastily printed out on A4 and stuck on otherwise respectable display stands. A group of men sit on melamine chairs outside the door to the bar, as one of their sons – almost buried under a huge pile of Lego – builds a replica of the Alexanderplatz television tower, complete with flashing lights. From a long booth running along an inside wall, volunteers from the Chaos Computer Club give out programmes and directions, and sell badges and stickers menaced with the club's distinctive horned skull and crossbones logo.

I've already missed the opening speaker, so instead of heading to the central lecture hall, I decide to check out the fringe presentations that take place in the smaller rooms. I enter the "lightning talks" room, a side hall populated with the same bland melamine chairs, half full. It's here that I'm greeted by my first surprise: it looks like the conference has no wi-fi. I can't help but feel that this is some elaborate joke played by one of the participants. A hacker con with no internet is like a garden show with no soil. Did someone break the connection? And why can't these magic hackers make some internet for themselves?

The compere is struggling through using someone's 3G dongle – lightning talks are open to anyone with something interesting to say that takes no longer than five minutes, and the entire programme exists only on the conference wiki, so without some kind of internet, he'd really have to wing it. The compere is chatting to the audience informally as he finalises the schedule and previews some of what's coming up. "I've just got a text message from Hans. He's stuck outside without a ticket, but hopefully he can hack his way in somehow. Let's give him until the end of the day", says the compere, as he moves the talk to the bottom of the list. I start to feel a bit more like I belong here – didn't I already hack my way in?

"We have a girl speaking", announces the compere, as he highlights one of the talks coming up. A cheer comes from the 95% male audience. However welcome women are to join this group of open-minded but slightly awkward men, few take up the offer. The compere punishes his keyboard and behind him on the projector screen we see the blink of green text on black. I realise that he's editing the lightning talks programme *in the command line*. I'm impressed.

Most ordinary people never interface with their computer like this, but hackers spend much of their time in the command line. If you're using a computer running Windows XP, here's how to try the command line out for size. Hit the start menu and select "*Run...*" on the righthand side. Then enter "cmd" in the dialogue box, and hit OK. The program that pops up is the command line interface. Try typing some commands, like "ping www.google.com" or "exit". There, don't you feel like a hacker?

The command line is the best place to see the conversation between man and machine taking place. Man speaks to the computer using a variety of truncated dialects (programming languages with names like Perl, Python and BASIC) that are designed to give their human speaker total control of the machine. The machine responds to each command, often filling up the screen with its own green text in response. No pictures, no mouse. But it's not really the place for editing documents, or checking your email. Unless, that is, you are a super geek.

"80% of people don't like their jobs. I turn off TVs for a living and I love my job."

The compere is finished setting up and the lightning talks have begun. The man speaking is Mitch Altman, inventor of

TV Be Gone, a universal remote control. At six foot four with Mohawk dreads and a thick Californian accent, Mitch doesn't look like the kind of guy who watches much TV. But the point of TV Be Gone is not to replace the remote control in your own home. It's to surreptitiously turn off TVs in public places. TV Be Gone has one button on it – the off-switch.

It goes unsaid why this might be a good idea – the lightning talk is mostly to pitch the micro-electronics lab Mitch will be running in the basement throughout the congress. But I know why I like it. Every time I visit London there are more TVs. The latest ones coat the walls of the escalator halls in the capital's most-used underground stations, making me long for the static paper ads I once found so intrusive.

Naomi Klein writes about the corporate takeover of "public" space in her best-selling anti-globalisation polemic *No Logo*. Mitch Altman's device is the logical (and slightly less risky) extension of the activities of urban guerrillas like Adbusters, who reclaim public space by making midnight alterations to the billboards of major brands in order to turn them into satirical art. When I was growing up, it was activism like this that looked most relevant to me. *No Logo* riffed off and egged on the anti-globalisation movement, a movement which saw street protests of revolutionary proportions every time the world's leaders descended on the cities of the economically dominant West to discuss global trade rules. Coca-Cola and Nike are this movement's bogey men, their crimes twofold: to take maximum advantage of the divide between the developed and developing world in order to drive up profits; to then use these profits to dominate culture across the world, hoovering up public art, public schools and public space, and refashioning them in their own corporate image.

My favourite slogan from this time is "Shopping is not creating", from Douglas Coupland's debut novel *Generation X*. And if there's a slogan that captures what draws me to places like the Chaos Congress, it is probably this one. To a lot of people, computers are the handmaidens of the corporate age – many will have encountered their first computer at work, and the networked communications infrastructure that powers the internet is also the oil in the machine of global business. Worse, personal computers and handheld devices – laptops, BlackBerrys, mobile phones – tether workers to their employers even while they are at home. The eighties personal computer gurus are often the same folk who went around major corporations advising them on ways to decouple their fortunes from those of their employees, ushering in the era of precarious employment that is my generation's norm. And yet, what's going on this weekend in Berlin is in a completely different place altogether. These guys certainly aren't shopping. And the stuff they're creating is pretty cool.

The lightning talks come thick and fast. One guy uses his five minutes to show the audience how he made himself a retro digital watch whose display looks like a game of Pong. The game the watch has been programmed to play is rigged – every hour, the bat on the left-hand side wins a point, and every minute, the bat on the right-hand side wins a point. Another guy shows how he broke the firmware on a disposable digital camera he bought for $10 to "liberate it" and turn it into a machine he could use again and again. Two Germans get up on stage and explain in stilted English their project to "democratise" digital radio – they're developing free software that will allow anyone to run a full radio transmission station using a laptop and one piece of hardware. And then it's someone else's turn – a guy in a balaclava silently shows the audience a video of himself turning a T-Mobile public phone booth into Doctor Who's TARDIS.

For some of these talks, the connection they have with computing would be lost on outsiders. But one moment serves to illustrate what joins them all together. A serious-looking Austrian is about to get his five minutes of fame (I forget on which topic) when, as he opens his laptop, the Microsoft start-up music sounds out across the hall. "Drum-di-da-drum. Da-dum." The audience erupts in jeers and the Austrian looks seriously flustered. His face makes it clear that someone has played a joke on him – he turns his laptop around so that the front few rows can confirm he's not running Windows. Because in this community Microsoft – commonly shortened to M$ – plays the role of bogey-man in the same way Nike and Coke do for the anti-globalisation movement.

In the outside world, the most memorable portrait of Bill Gates as a young man is the mugshot Albuquerque police captured of him after he was caught running a stop light on their watch, aged 22. But for the geek world, it is an article the founder of Microsoft and (until recently) richest man in the world wrote a year earlier, in 1976, called "An open letter to hobbyists". In it, he labelled people who were using the software he and colleagues at his new company Micro-Soft were developing as "thieves" and "parasites", demanding they pay royalties. Gates was the first person to try commercialising software for personal computers – up until that point writing software for early personal computers had been a hobbyists' pursuit, limited to a bedraggled band of academics and enthusiasts. But this culture of free exchange didn't wash well with Bill. He wanted to make money.

And of course, he did – more money than any single individual had ever made before, in fact. But while Microsoft was busy working towards getting a computer running their software on every desk in every home in the world, the hobbyists didn't just go away. Instead, from the mid-eighties onwards, they organised to create rival software and applications that they protected with legal licences that would ensure no-one could enclose them and start selling them exclusively and for profit. This so-called "free" software wasn't just free because it cost nothing, what hackers refer to as "free as in beer". It was "free as in freedom" too. It left early hackers at liberty to share and build on each other's work, and thus to make what they were building better than what Bill Gates was selling.

The software they created and the organisational methods and legal tools they used to do it would become defining features of the internet age. Most web-servers run not on Microsoft's software, but on free software. Google would not exist without free software. And the "open source" method of working that the pioneers of free software adopted has been used as a prism through which to view the properties of the web for at least a decade.

If Bill Gates had been completely in charge, there would be no world wide web. Sure, Gates saw that computers could play some role in home entertainment. About the time Tim Berners-Lee was circulating his ideas about the possibilities of linking documents together using something called hypertext, Gates was proposing set-top computers in every home, able to deliver more entertainment programming than even satellite TV. Gates initially missed the Web, because he couldn't see the people who bought his products as anything more than consumers. He didn't realise they were creators, too.

There's a reason the command line is so hidden in Windows – the company don't expect you to use it.

Of course, with creation comes destruction. I haven't really come here to see art projects – cool as they may be. I want to find some cracking. The lightning talks offer up a couple of titbits. One talk, entitled "cache games", shows how to manipulate someone else's computer from afar using the web caching system. Another details how to launch a distributed denial of service (DDoS) attack using peer-to-peer networks. If this was the magician's circle, then think of these guys as fairground conjurers. For the really good tricks, it's clear I'm going to have to leave the sideshows.

The main lecture hall is accessed from the first, and top floor of the Berliner. Its domed roof has something of the Biosphere 1 about it, but despite this, the lecture hall is pretty normal. Normal that is, until you look up on the stage.

It's another command-line screen, but this time, it's nearly ten feet wide, and is scrolling through green text almost too quickly to catch. The man operating the computer is Harald Welte, a German hacker in his late twenties dressed head to toe in black and with a matching helmet of brushed black hair. I lean across to the man sitting next to me.

"What's he doing?"

The man turns at me and smiles: "He's sniffing all the mobile phones in the audience, trying to find one he can break into."

At this moment, the screen stops scrolling. The last line on it shows a phone has been penetrated, and lists its number. "Send message?", it asks. The audience cheers. I know it's not my number, but I reach into my handbag anyway. I quickly switch off my phone, just in case. Welte keeps scrolling.

This is how the Chaos Communication Congress made international media headlines the year I was there: it demonstrated for the first time how to hack the mobile phone networking protocol, the Global System for Mobile Communications, or GSM for short. Unlike computer networks, there aren't that many hackers into playing with breaking mobile phone networks. There are a bunch of reasons for this – while computers were originally designed to be modified by their users, mobile phone handsets weren't, and the fact that only a handful of corporations manufacture handsets means this isn't going to change anytime soon. Also, the networking protocols used by mobile phones mean that manipulating traffic is that much harder. Think of mobile phones like Bill Gates' ideal internet. Built for consumers, not creators.

Harald Welte has been working with a small group of hackers to change this because, as he puts it, "do you want to be the 100,000th person to do some TCP/IP fuzzing, or the 10th person to do some GSM fuzzing?" (fuzzing is basically bombarding a computer system with random data, to see if it crashes). As a well-paid security researcher he can invest serious money in his hobby, and lately he's been buying mobile phone base stations off eBay. Out of these, and using the reams of documentation about protocol standards available from manufacturers in dusty parts of the web, he's building his own mobile phone network. It's even running this weekend at CCC, and legally: he's obtained an experimental licence from Germany's telecommunications regulator.

Beyond the simple fun of it, Welte isn't explicit about why he's doing this. But it's true to say that once he's able to replicate a commercial mobile network, he'll be able to work out better ways to crack it.

It's not Welte, however, who makes headlines, but a cryptographer called Karsten Nohl. Karsten's presentation "GSM: SRSLY?" is a summary of work he and colleagues have been publicly engaged in since the August Hacking at Random conference Rop Gonggrijp helps organise in the Netherlands, when he made his intention to crack the standard clear. The hack has come good: after several hundred man hours have been put into constructing rainbow tables, the weak cryptography that protects the standard has been cracked. The implications are serious – a fairly simply hack has turned the world's network of over three billion GSM mobile phones into the most widely deployed privacy threat on the planet. Karsten is offhand as he underlines the implications of his work in the introduction to his talk:

> Cloning, spoofing, man-in-the-middle, decrypting, sniffing, crashing, DoS'ing, or just plain having fun. If you can work a BitTorrent client and a standard GNU build process then you can do it all, too. Prepare to change the way you look at your cell phone, forever.

If all this sounds like bragging jargon, then listen to how the BBC report the breakthrough: "The work could allow anyone - including criminals - to eavesdrop on private phone conversations". In reply, the body responsible for maintaining and developing the GSM standard, the GSM Association, accused Nohl of being commercially motivated and hinted that the work he'd undertaken to break the standard was "highly illegal". They dismissed the vulnerabilities identified by Nohl.

I've finally caught up with Rop Gonggrijp, and I'm sitting in the press room with my dictaphone in front of him. He's shorter than I remember him, but also more handsome. Campaigning together, I remember him relentlessly picking me up on things he thought I could have done better. At the time, I ascribed his arrogance to the dual ego of hacker and millionaire (Rop started the Netherlands' first ISP, XS4ALL, in the mid-nineties, selling it on to Dutch Telecom a few years later). Here among his fellow hackers, his "family", he is infinitely more relaxed, and actually quite charming.

Spats between hackers and vendors like the ones between Karsten Nohl and the GSM Association are familiar to Rop. He's been trespassing on commercial electronic voting machinery and seeing if he can break it since 2006. Over time, hackers have come to agree that this is the best way to expose security vulnerabilities on behalf of the millions of non-geeks who use commercial computer products to bank, vote, travel, identify themselves or communicate. While vendors might like to practice "security through obscurity", the hackers haven't let them. In what can be viewed as a microcosm of society that contains only the people – vendors and hackers – who can really drill down into how a particular technology actually works, the public vigilantism of hackers such as Karsten Nohl keeps the vendors honest. At least that's the theory.

"We had this discussion at congress in the first ten years that I was part of it," explains Rop, "What's a good security policy? Should we be forcing vendors to change their stuff by publicly disclosing vulnerabilities? Or should we just let them fix it in peace? That debate has ended. Everybody agrees that full disclosure is the way to go and that these vendors will never get off their asses by themselves. That's official government policy, nobody disagrees. Not even the vendors disagree."

What's helped hackers at CCC and elsewhere win this argument has been the rapidly growing importance of digital technology in everybody's lives.

"Twenty-two years ago this was very much a pirate gathering. Highly repressed. Authorities were doing searches at people's homes even though they didn't understand who we were or what we did... All the political issues that we associated ourselves with didn't exist yet. There was a sense that there needed to be freedom, there was a sense that there was a new world looming over the horizon, that these networks were going to be big and that computer security would be important and that the only solution for that was transparency. So those seeds were there but to be telling random passers-by that these issues had any importance to anybody but us was next to impossible. People thought 'Yes these are interesting issues for your community, I'm sure.' Just like the fishing community has interesting issues about what bait to use. But you would not be able to convince people that this would be important to them, that they would one day be on the network."

As this year's GSM hack demonstrates, those days are now gone. If the cryptography that protects our mobile phone conversations isn't up to the job, that is, if all it takes to pluck them out of the air and eavesdrop on them is a little technical skill, then we're all at risk. And of course it's not just our phones we need to worry about. Rop continues, "I guess the biggest change is that people have become familiar with these issues because they touch their lives. It's now recognised that we were just the first to be there. These issues are now mainstream. Whether or not you can put something on the internet, the whole issue of digital copies, all these issues are now mainstream issues and they interest many more people than just us."

To a hacker, architecture is politics: how you build something will dictate how it will get used. The rest of the world is just getting used to this concept with regard to buildings. Watching the demolition of sixties tower blocks that had dictated community life in my one-time neighbourhood of East London I knew that this was a political act, a confession, that old ways of thinking about welfare provision and social justice had been forced to change by the failure of sixties idealism. But I'm not sure that outside of the group of specialists gathered at CCC people think of computers and computer programs as having "architecture" at all, much less architecture that somehow embodies or dictates a political reality. And as for this army of volunteer building inspectors breaking and entering to evaluate said architecture, outside of the occasional newspaper headline, they are pretty much invisible. And that's how they like it.

Volunteers working for the public good, with or without the public's consent. This is how the attendees of 26C3 see themselves. At least, this is how they are prepared to talk about themselves when forced to go on the record. Off the record, more than one hacker confesses to me over the course of my weekend in Berlin that what he really likes doing is causing trouble. This hardly comes as a surprise – the language used by GSM hackers Nohl and Welte shows they derive some glee from what they do. "I like making trouble, and so I make smart trouble," confides one hacker. "It's taken me a while to realise this, but now I'm older I would even go so far as to say that my politics comes second. I pick it because it helps me justify the trouble I make."

The lectures at CCC finish at 2am – hackers, according to Rop, are people with no "night rhythm", so the after midnight slot is the most coveted for potential speakers. But the conference has succumbed to its own success, and to the success of its participants in securing entry no matter how many signs are put up saying the event has sold out. The main lecture hall is packed, it's strictly one in/one out, and nobody's coming out. I decide I need a change of scene.

I'm headed to c-Base, Berlin's Groucho for geeks. Outside, it's been snowing. Orange traffic lights suspended high on electric wires sway in the evening breeze, and the halogen street lights shine yellow on the slush. I take a wide Soviet avenue headed back to what once was West Berlin. I've only the directions of one of CCC's Engels to guide me. I'm to turn left as soon as I cross the river, which I do, but it doesn't look promising.

Just as I'm about to give up, I hear a group, two girls and a guy, coming up behind me, speaking French. At first, I assume they have nothing to do with CCC – they're too fashionably dressed. But then one of them calls my name and I realise it's Jérémie Zimmerman, a French internet campaigner I used to work with when I ran the Open Rights Group. He delivered a lecture at CCC today, on plans he claims that the European Commission are hatching to "privatise" the internet, to turn it into a glorified pay-TV service. As spokesperson for La Quadrature du Net, the French campaign for a free and open internet, he is one of the most energetic and effective campaigners on digital civil rights working in Europe today. Unlike many overworked activists, he's also great fun to be around, and he eagerly lets me join his party on the way to c-Base. As we push past some foliage up a mud path away from the river I'm relieved to have found someone who knows his way around. As soon as we get close to the door, a thumping bass line beckons us inside. It's a long time since I've been to a nightclub, and I'm keen to get inside.

Going to nightclubs used to be my job. For about two years I sent dispatches from the dance floor to trendy London music magazines: interviews with monosyllabic DJs, record and club reviews. The whole experience gave me a fairly jaded view of the club scene, which more and more seemed to me a commercial imposter, an automaton occupying the cadaver of the criminalised underground rave and free party movement. It was all air-kissing and VIP rooms. I go to bed early these days.

As we file past the man on the door and enter c-Base, I get a familiar feeling of being on edge. This might actually be *cool*. Girls with big eyes and undercuts moon past my line of sight as we do the first tour of the club. We head down a set of rickety spiral stairs, looking for the bar. Instead, we find people sat around on junk-shop sofas, skinning up joints. Not our scene – we loop back up the stairs.

Back on the main floor, a Bacchic kind of trance thumps out from the soundsystem, behind which another girl with an undercut (and geeky glasses) is doing the DJing. A remodelled arcade machine sits at one end of the busy bar – looking closer I see it's been hacked in order to make it offer almost every arcade game from the eighties to play for free, using an arcade machine emulator set-up called MAME. More geek kudos is offered by a ten-foot square touchscreen that nestles next to the entrance to another long corridor, leading to the cloakroom. But these touches are subtle – at face, this looks like any hip nightclub in East London.

The c-Base has its own mythology, explains Jérémie as we queue to check our coats. According to stories, a space station called c-Base is buried underneath Berlin city centre, having crash-landed by mistake here after a particularly bumpy exit from a time warp. Evidence of this is Alexanderplatz's menacing tower, actually the space station's antenna repurposed by the Soviets after they discovered the station wreckage. Many more parts of the c-Base station are in the hands of elite scientists. The c-Base club is actually constructed from one module of the space station.

It's a tall tale, of course, but I'm pleased to see geeks having a giggle at themselves. The real legacy of the c-Base is still important. c-Base is one of the first hack spaces, multifunctional workshops with the relaxed door policy of squats yet stocked with tools and bandwidth. It has inspired hundreds of others across the world.

I decide to lose the others and take a look around. A small door at the back is marked "VIPs only", an offer I can't refuse. Inside, two large rooms are empty of people, but full of soldering irons, wires, electronics boards and dead monitors. It looks like something from a Caro-Jeunet film, and just as creepy – I know already that I don't belong here. As if to confirm it, a voice asks me from the shadows – "can I help you?"

"Sorry, I'm in the wrong place," I stutter, and head back to the crowd outside.

chapter

Courage is Contagious

Chapter 2: Courage is contagious

"Somehow," Rop tells me, "the Chaos Computer Club has managed to attract new debates and it's been able to capture the new things that are going on. Jimmy Wales was here when Wikipedia was really young. Everybody understands that this club tries to find the new issues. And the people coming to the club are those interested in thinking five years ahead. What's going to happen next?"

What indeed. It's day two of the conference, and I'm pretty sure that the talk I'm waiting to watch is the main event this year. It hasn't got anything to do with GSM, or mobile phones, and it won't make headlines for a little while yet. But when it does, it will make them all over the world.

Julian Assange and Daniel Schmitt take to the stage. They're here as spokespeople for WikiLeaks, the whistle-blowing website that has published over one million leaked documents since its founding in 2007. In that short time, WikiLeaks has been behind more scoops than the *Washington Post* has notched up in 30 years. In the UK in 2009, it was at the centre of two major news stories. The first was about the use of libel law to gag reporting about a company who had dumped toxic waste illegally off the coast of Cote d'Ivoire leaving thousands of locals sick and at least a dozen dead. The scandal led to serious initiatives to reform libel laws in the UK. The second, when WikiLeaks published over 1,000 emails sent over a period of ten years between scientists at the Climatic Research Institute in Norwich, UK, pretty much derailed international talks on climate change the following month in Copenhagen. WikiLeaks has broken stories of similar national and international importance in Venezuela, Peru, Kenya, the United States and Mexico. And in Iceland they are national heroes, after they published records showing exactly which of Iceland's banking elite withdrew all their funds from the failed bank Kaupthing days before it collapsed in 2008.

Now WikiLeaks have a plan. They're going to use their new friends in the Icelandic Parliament to persuade Iceland's leaders to rebuild their nation as a "Switzerland of bits", a haven for squirreling away digital information out of reach of those governments that would "tax" it with censorship. It helps that Iceland's cold – the server farms it will have to run in order to fulfil this international role will need a lot of cooling.

Their new idea sounds barmy, but WikiLeaks already operates different servers in different locations in Europe and Africa in order to take advantage of a patchwork of laws – about protecting sources, about libel, about copyright – which together make their operation legally watertight. For example, servers hosted in Sweden handle all contact with sources, because Sweden has an excellent source-protection law. All Iceland would need to do is sew these laws together and pass them in one bundle, and WikiLeaks could move its whole operation there.

It's an intriguing approach, some might say crazy in its ambition. And it's definitely a hacker's approach. Free speech campaigners generally like talking (that much is obvious) but for all the good they do, they don't actually do much. WikiLeaks is *all* doing. It takes the problem of suppression of speech and, rather than "highlighting" it or "raising awareness", it applies a slightly messy but acceptable solution – what in computer programming terms might be called a "patch". "Okay," WikiLeaks says, "would the world work a bit better like this?"

Unsurprisingly, it's also an approach which goes down very well with this audience. Hackers are used to getting results: in fact, they often describe this as one of the most compelling reasons for spending a lifetime with computers. In the command line, results are immediate, and dominion is clear. General purpose programmable computers may be powerful things, and to the average user they may often appear more powerful than us. But for the hacker who has the knowledge to control his machine, it is the ultimate creative tool. The way this skill allows him to make his mark on the world becomes addictive. It seems natural, then, that the hacker should begin to seek this same fix in other spheres.

Understand this, and you are halfway to understanding radical hacker culture. To understand the other half, you need to look to the power of the network. It was this power – underwritten by connectivity provided by the nascent 'net - that allowed volunteer coders to club together and create the free software that underpins Google, Amazon and the rest of the popular web. Somewhere inside the heart of every member of the audience at 26c3 is the hope that this same power can be harnessed for political causes. "If more people have just half the courage of some of the WikiLeaks volunteers, then the world would be a better place," says Daniel. "Well," he goes on, "We think courage is contagious".

This final call to arms earns the two WikiLeaks men a five-minute standing ovation. I find I'm on my feet as well. But as much as I'm participating in what has essentially turned into something more like a prayer meeting, I'm also curious. For one thing, I'm intrigued to see anyone associating themselves with WikiLeaks at all. When the organisation launched, it made its representatives very hard to find, and although I know friends of mine from Open Rights Group days have advised WikiLeaks, I've never met anyone before who claims to run it. I'm here to learn about hackers, not journalists, but something about this presentation makes me want to know more. Who are these men and what are the philosophies that drive them? How, and how clearly, do they define the boundaries between privacy and free speech when they're deciding what to publish? And, perhaps most importantly, what are they hoping to achieve?

After a little obfuscation, and a lot of vetting, Assange and Schmitt agree separately to be interviewed. The interviews turn out to reveal two very different characters indeed. But then I suppose I should have expected an organisation that believes in the power of unfettered information to transform society not to be too worried about presenting a unified party line.

"Ask yourself, why aren't there more journalists in the West being killed?"

Julian Assange is a pale man, white skin, white hair. Etiolated, pale like a plant that's been kept in an airing cupboard. His gentle Australian accent that sings up and down just adds to this impression of pallor, and he has the soft, untouched hands and well-manicured, but slightly too-long (for a boy) fingernails I associate with acid dealers, accountants and hackers.

It turns out that, as I suspected, he's the latter. In 1992, aged 24, Julian was convicted of more than 20 counts of computer crimes in an Australian court. In 1999 he registered the domain leaks.org, but it has only been recently that the idea of WikiLeaks has really taken off, thanks to what he terms, "a particular intersection of economic forces and understanding".

Julian Assange talks this way quite a lot. One word he uses again and again is "fiscalisation". It's a term he uses in opposition to "politics". Western journalists, he says, have been "fiscalised": that's why they're not doing their jobs anymore, which in turn is why fewer of them are getting killed. I ask him to define what he means by "fiscalisation".

"It's where power relationships are exercised through contracts and bank transfers, options and shares. So if there's a change in political mood it doesn't matter because it doesn't change the values on contracts, it doesn't change the numbers in banks. Power interests have put their wealth into a structure which is immune, not totally but mostly, from political sanctions."

It seems to me that what Julian is talking about is the triumph of global capitalism over Western democracy, the slow-knit of the corporate ethos into civic life. "In the West," he continues, "Perhaps speech is free because it actually has very little ability to change underlying power dynamics. Whereas in the developing world the basic structure of society is political and so when the political mood changes, who has power and who has assets can completely change." In such a context, most Western journalists choose to play along, "I guess Western journalists start to become comfortable once they have some influence. They start to become comfortable and they don't want to lose it. And they can still have access to high levels of political power without taking risks, they can still go to all the right cocktail parties without taking risks. There are some exceptions to this but there's not many."

When I ask Daniel why he thinks WikiLeaks has scored more scoops than the *Washington Post* in its short history, his answers are much more down-to-earth. Not everyone with something interesting to leak will necessarily know who to speak to, he argues, and those that do might not trust journalists to protect them or to make the best use of the material.

"We offer a service to anyone that feels motivated, right at the moment where their motivation is at its peak, in the sense that they can go online and just do it," he explains, "It's built by success. People see that somebody else entrusted us with something that might have screwed them over if it went wrong, and it worked out. And the more good examples there are where this works out for people I guess the more people will rely on us."

Daniel seems a lot less ready to criticise the mainstream media than Julian, but he does admit that, "for various reasons", there's a gap in investigative journalism. It's an expensive investment, he says, and he sees WikiLeaks as "a complementary effort to try and make it cheap again".

Both men are aware that a part of their future lies in partnering with the press. For Daniel, the key realisation working with WikiLeaks is that "things given away for free are not worth anything. By creating scarcity you somehow create value". Early experiments with offering exclusive access to material to particular newspapers have produced mixed results, but WikiLeaks will continue to trial this approach. And despite their fiscalised state, Julian also understands the value journalists offer WikiLeaks:

"Contextualisation, adapting something to a local community or a political mood at that particular moment, making it emotional and hyping it up: these are very important things that journalists do."

Although Daniel strikes me as the more pragmatic of the two WikiLeaks men, his business-like approach belies a radical ideological commitment to free speech. Perhaps more the consummate spokesperson than Julian, when I ask Daniel where he draws the line between privacy and free speech, he is keen to stress that his answer reflects his own personally-held views, and not the views of WikiLeaks.

Daniel believes that now we're living in a global world, now the decisions we make every day have ramifications in regions of the world utterly remote to us, we need to be fully informed. He paraphrases a famous quote from Alexander Solzhenitsyn's Nobel Prize lecture:

"The only solution to the problems we have in society is that everything is everyone's business. The key to the information society," he continues, "is that we have to actually care about the information we have, so that we go from a world that we live in right now, where we expect politicians and the media to filter things for us, to a society where we actually want to know. One of the proofs of being global enough to survive in the long run is that you actually care, that you're not just deciding to outsource the responsibility, the knowledge and everything to someone who is taking the decision for you. But that you actually participate again. It's going from a spectator sport to participating in the game. And if you don't, you'll just be sitting there watching it until it's over and that's it, basically."

When it comes to privacy, he goes on, we're asking the wrong question. Instead we should be looking at our emotional capacity towards others. He talks about a trade-off "between not being too interested in what your neighbour is doing and maybe understanding that something terrible is happening". He talks about the consequences of WikiLeaks releasing a list of members of the British National Party in 2008: "The question is what do you do, what do you make out of it? Do you torch your neighbour's car because you understand that he's a BNP member? Or do you maybe start talking to him when you meet him on the street? From my perspective everyone is entitled to his political views, that is his private business. But if those views have implications for me as a person in this society, then I need to understand what maybe we have to change in this world in order to not grow people that are hateful towards others."

Julian's approach to the same issue starts with the information itself and not the people to whom the information pertains. "There is a universe of bits," he explains, "All the possible information that human beings individually have access to that have not necessarily turned public yet. Some of those bits have a civilising effect on our life on earth. So the question becomes: how do you find those bits? I say a very good economic signal is that certain organisations spend economic effort in suppressing those bits and making sure those bits are not public. And the degree of reform effect that those bits may have is broadly in proportion to the degree of economic effort that is spent on suppressing that material. Why else would you want to suppress it?"

It sounds like a question he actually wants me to answer, so I do. I suggest that this is exactly the sort of public interest argument used by the paparazzi and the gutter press. The conversation takes a surprising turn.

"I've never heard that argument used in relation to paparazzi," Julian replies "But I can see that maybe that's true. However, I'm a great supporter of the paparazzi. I think the concern with paparazzi is a fairly disgusting, liberal, middle class preoccupation with saying that all the interests of the proletariat are debased."

Julian brings up the so-called "phone-hacking" scandal. "This *News of the World* thing with this using a default password on a couple of celebrities' voicemail boxes to listen to some of the voicemails that they were receiving. So was this a terrible, terrible thing? Of course it wasn't a terrible, terrible thing. Now there's a law of the land and if the land says you shouldn't listen to people's voicemails, then of course the people who did listen to this directly should be treated equally under the law. But is it a terrible, terrible thing that a newspaper took that end product and maybe didn't look too hard into how private investigators were acquiring this material? Not at all. These celebrities were wielding their influence on the public and that's why the public were interested in them. And if they're unhappy with that, well they can stop trying to live different private lives to public lives."

What Julian objects to most about the *News of the World* voicemail intercepts, it seems, is the ramifications the scandal will have for regulation of the press. "In Peru we released over 60 telephone intercepts of politicians speaking to businessmen. It was the biggest political event in Peru this year, and was on all five major dailies' front pages. These were actual telephone intercepts. These weren't voicemail boxes," here you can feel the hacker's disdain that the voicemail intercepts should be called "hacks" at all, "So I feel that it was just disgraceful that the *Guardian* wasted its time on that issue. All they ended up doing was producing a climate that increased the amount of regulation of investigative journalism. I mean, the jumping up and down about the fact that the *News of the World* was not actually just reprinting an AP newswire or stealing something from somewhere else or reprinting a press release, but they'd actually done original investigative work about people in this society that their readers were genuinely interested in."

If Daniel is the more humanitarian, optimistic of the two WikiLeaks men, then when it comes to the media, I think Julian is certainly the more savvy. He understands and accepts the way journalists choose to sensationalise news. "What a lot of journalists do is start a fight. If you're a journalist, you ring up one power group and you say, 'Hey, what do you think about this document? Doesn't this imply that you're a pack of bastards?' And they say, 'No, no, no. Actually it's not like that.' And then you call up another power group and you say, 'Hey, doesn't this document imply that these other guys are a pack of bastards?' And they say, 'Yes, absolutely. They are a pack of bastards.' Then you go back to the first group and you say, 'Hey, the second group says you're a pack of bastards.' And so now you've got a fight that has just happened that day and that's a conflict between major power groups. And human beings are naturally and rightfully interested in fights between power."

So, I ask, WikiLeaks must sometimes play that role in the story?

"In some cases, sure. We become part of the fight and we have actually, of course, used our entry into one of those fights in order to draw attention to the material itself. In some cases, many cases, no-one's interested in the material until people try and sue us about it."

Nonetheless, perhaps mindful of the treatment people get when they launch themselves into the public sphere, Julian seems keen to keep his profile out of it, and refuses to answer any questions that would reveal more about his personal life.

"I can understand why people like to build personal profiles," he explains, "It can be actually very helpful in pushing your ideas. But it's not my character to do that."

I leave the conference centre with my head spinning. I've arranged to meet some old friends from university at a bar downtown near the aptly named Hackershemarket. If you had no money and were into art, Berlin was a great place to be in the noughties. Housing was super cheap, welfare and tenancy law was on your side, and the city was – and still is – full of pirate nightclubs, galleries and art spaces. This couple both study history of art: he's about to get his PhD; hers has won her a permanent fellowship at Berlin's Humboldt University. He wears pointy shoes, she wears vintage dresses bought by weight in downtown East Berlin. They have a Siamese cat called Raoul. Neither of them care about computers, although they both have Apple Mac laptops for work. Their names are Sarah and Luke.

The one problem with Berlin, they tell me, is the Germans. They're all so bloody rude. To prove their point, Sarah and Luke have brought me to what seems like the most poorly-served bar in Berlin. When the waitress does eventually arrive at our table, it seems she has only done so in order to let us know that tonight she shouldn't really be working at all – the boss has brought her in because he got the rota wrong. We commiserate with her, and decide it might be in our interests to offer her a consolatory drink. At least that way we might be more likely to get one ourselves.

I hadn't intended to, but I invite Sarah and Luke back to Chaos with me. I want to see the scene through their eyes. Obviously, the way I've described it – I'm still living my narrative that this is the last bastion of cultural rebellion in the Western world – they're desperate to come. It's only as we're on our way back to Chaos – after several drinks commiserating with our waitress – that I realise that the way I see it might not be the way they see it. What if it's just a room full of weird-looking men?

I sneak Sarah and Luke back in with me (hack #2!). We do two circuits of the venue – one upstairs and one downstairs, and at first I'm regretting ever bringing them here. In their hipster gear, they stand out badly. And they're treating this place like a zoo – Sarah, wide-eyed, points and gasps as men in full-length leather trench coats with pink hair walk past. We duck into a side lecture – a critique of computer theories that draws on intellectuals who are deeply unfashionable to my PoMo friends. We somehow sneak in to the main lecture hall. The talk is impenetrably technical. I decide to give my vision one last try on the uninitiated. We head down to the basement.

I haven't talked much about the basement and that's because I'm not meant to. I sat here with Rop on day one, and we agreed that no other room in Europe would at this very moment house so many people on the autistic spectrum as this one. The basement is where the hacking happens. Low lights, empty doughnut boxes and drinks cans. Laptops, soldering irons, motherboards. Make your own wi-fi adapter so you need never pay for internet on the move again. Hack the system.

Off the hack space is Chaos' very own nightclub, two rooms in the conference centre that appear to have escaped Germany's recent smoking ban, and that pump out Berlin techno all day and all night. On a trio of borrowed sofas balance at least two-dozen red-eyed hackers – I see Julian throned in the centre, deep in conversation. Eventually, Sarah, Luke and I sit down on a spare square metre of the pulsating floor, and roll up some cigarettes. The only way to beat the toxic smoke cloud is to add to it, it would seem. Smoking's been banned for less than three years back in England, and already I'm so used to my clean, safe, indoor air that this feels dirty.

We took the walk through the hack space at a fast pace, my fear – that my noobie guests would reach down and peer at the wrong secret project and get us into trouble – goading me on. But the flash of blinking lights and hackers crouched over electronics in dark recesses seems to have changed Sarah and Luke's mood. I think they are beginning to buy my story that this is a radical space. Perhaps the techno's helping.

Luke leans over to me. "How many of the people here are working undercover for the secret service?" he asks. I know where he's coming from. It's said that radical American political groups in the sixties often found once they had been disbanded that half their members were CIA. The truth is that lots of the men getting high in this room at 2am on a Sunday after Christmas are likely to have equally high level security clearance. The clients that care most about top quality computer security are governments and banks, and to work for them, they first need to check you out. But even though some of these folk must surely work for the security services, that doesn't necessarily make them spies, more poachers turned gamekeepers. Still, given some of the amoral attitudes I've encountered at the conference this year, if the government – any government – required them to make trouble that was more interesting than anything else on offer, I've no doubt at least some of them would accept the invitation.

Is hacking just a murky subculture? Or is it a counterculture, maybe even a political movement?

"You can't be a counterculture forever without becoming irrelevant." Rop and I are sitting on a set of steps leading up to the sound booth that controls the main lecture hall, enjoying our aerial view of Chaos. He goes on: "If there is some truth to what you say, if you have an argument and you're smart, you should be able to convince other people that you're right. And if you are, you're going to be a political movement, not a counterculture any more. We've been around for 25 years and, given that, we'd better be a political movement. If you stamp your foot on the ground and you say, 'I am a force to be reckoned with and

I have some arguments here that may carry some weight,' and you stay a counterculture, you're doing something wrong."

But if the sixties are anything to go by, aren't the legacies of such movements just deeply disappointing? Compared to what they promised at the outset – community, liberty, psychedelic enlightenment – the age of globalisation, consumerism and societal breakdown that followed the sixties looks like a bum deal to me. Will next generations compare the hacker ethos against what it eventually wrought on the political mainstream and find it to come up wanting? Are the positive, intended effects of hacker culture enough to outweigh the negative, unintended effects? Is Rop prepared, I wonder, for the next generation to look back on the hacker counterculture and see that it failed?

"Oh sure." says Rop, "Nobody's perfect."

chapter 3

information wants to be FREE

Chapter 3: Information wants to be free

"What's wrong with the corporate world? I don't get what's wrong with consumerism and I don't get what's wrong with corporations per se."

Stewart Brand is sitting across from me in the small private living room of a central London hotel. At 72, he's looking remarkably well, although the trip over here from his hometown of Sausalito, California – where he lives on a tugboat with his wife – has taken its toll on his voice. We've already had to reschedule this interview once – the publicist for his current book was worried he might overdo it, and his slot on Radio 4's *Start the Week* was certainly gravelish. Liver spots pepper an expansive forehead revealed by several decades of hair loss. But his eyes are bright, and his old world courtesy combines well with his check shirt, leather waistcoat and slacks. I'm feeling very comfortable sitting across from him on a cosy sofa, as a particularly violent bout of January weather rages in the city outside.

Brand is a 1960s original. When Tom Wolfe first came across him as one of Ken Kesey's Merry Pranksters, madly driving a souped-up pickup through the streets of San Francisco, he recorded the encounter thus:

> Stewart Brand, a thin blonde guy with a blazing disk on his forehead too, and a whole necktie made of Indian beads. No shirt, however, just an Indian bead necktie on bare skin and a white butcher's coat with medals from the King of Sweden on it.

Brand comes from a world I dreamed about in my teens, one I searched for through celluloid and print. A world where Steppenwolf growl "You know I smoked a lot of grass. Oh Lord! I popped a lot of pills. But I've never touched nothin' that my spirit couldn't kill", just as two men release the kickstands from under their motorcycles, throw their watches into the Nevada dust and set off across America to New Orleans in my favourite film, *Easy Rider*. But Brand isn't just any old hippy, he's also the missing link between the lost world of sixties counterculture and the radical values of the 21st century hacker.

It's a complex legacy. There's no doubt that today's rampant consumer culture took its cue from the radical individualism promoted by the navel-gazing hippy liberals of sixties West Coast America. What's less known but equally certain is that these very same hippies were a driving force in the development of personal computer and internet culture. In so being, they bequeathed my generation – or at least the folk who know enough to make it to the Chaos Congress each year – the tools and the vision we would one day employ in an attempt to reboot that culture, to turn consumers back into participants.

When I was 19, Ken Kesey came to my home town, Brighton, along with a reproduction of Furthur, the psychedelic school bus he and the Merry Pranksters first drove around the US in the late sixties on one long trip funded by the proceeds of selling Kesey's film rights for *One Flew Over the Cuckoo's Nest.* It was that journey that Tom Wolfe immortalised in *The Electric Kool-Aid Acid Test.* Thirty years later in 1999, some of the original Merry Pranksters came with him to the Peace Statue on Brighton Beach – the electrical whizz kid Babbs, Mountain Girl – but Brand, the man sitting in front of me now, who travelled in Kesey's inner circle in the sixties, was not among them. In nineties' Brighton, Kesey came off to me as a rainbow-clad kids TV presenter past his prime – not surprising, given that the legacy of sixties psychedelic culture was perhaps felt strongest in eighties' children's TV. And as for the experience, I remember being just a little non-plussed. As Wolfe might have put it, I did not get "on the bus" that day. I think it was when I saw some familiar branding and realised the trip was being sponsored by Channel 4 that I cut my losses and turned away.

In 1966, Brand put on the TRIPS festival, one of the first public "acid tests". The event serves as Wolfe's narrative apex as he charts the rise and fall of psychedelic culture in *...Acid Test.* At it, the Grateful Dead and Big Brother & the Holding Company (a few months before they enlisted their iconic lead vocalist, Janis Joplin) play against fantastic light shows to "the heads", who are "pouring in by the hundreds, bombed out of their gourds"

In the nights before the party, while planning the festival at Brand's apartment in North Beach, Kesey racks up his second charge for marijuana possession, an inconvenience that would see him forced underground – paranoid and on the run – in the following months. But the party itself was a blast, and what's more, it grossed over $12,000. He may have been a hippy, but Stewart Brand was good at making money.

I'm not quite sure how I inspired the anti-anti-corporate rant Brand has just finished, but it serves to illustrate the time that stretches between his generation and mine. Whereas Brand's generation had the military-industrial complex of the Cold War to haunt their nightmares, the politically conscious and privileged young hipsters of today are more likely to be found protesting Big Oil, Big Coal and Big Pharma. If there is a movement as obviously exuberant as the hippy movement today, you'll probably find it incubating at Arms Trade demos, tooling-up at Climate Camp, and bursting onto the streets of whichever city the global leaders of the capitalist world choose to meet in each year.

These days, Brand will more likely be seen on the other side of the security cordon, advising the companies these young radicals are protesting against. "The thing I mainly resist," Brand elaborates, "is that all consumerism is bad or all corporations are bad. It's just, nothing useful has been said yet. And in fact, the opposite of something useful has been done because it prevents further thought or further investigation or further pursuing of the actual situation".

In the late eighties, Brand founded the Global Business Network along with two former executives from Royal Dutch/Shell. Described as "a company/think tank/men's club whose explicit purpose is to shape the future of the world", the company's clients include major American utility firms like Pacific Gas and Electric, Nissan, AT&T, Universal and ABC. And the US military. As Brand tells me: "GBN happily does a lot of work with the national security people and the intelligence community in the US, who I love working for because they're smart, engaged, serious public servants."

"We blew it.", says Captain America to Billy in *Easy Rider* – the last piece of dialogue before the two of them get shot off their bikes by a Southern hick on the highway heading home from New Orleans. "WE BLEW IT!" chant Ken Kesey's Merry Pranksters a year earlier in the final lines of Tom Wolfe's novel. Well, the acid must have been good, if it helped them see that far into the future.

But the acid turned out not to be that good, and that's really the point of this interview. "I started using psychedelic drugs earlier than most and I stopped using psychedelic drugs earlier than most people started using them actually," Brand laughs, "I had my last LSD in 1969, not because somebody shook their finger at me but because I was tired of bum trips. And I saw people trying to cure their personality problems with LSD, which was exacerbating their problems, rather than curing them. And so I thought, 'Well, OK. Something is self-limiting here and I think I'll just not bother with it anymore.' That turned out to be the right thing to have done and lots of people went through various forms of that."

Despite his generation's conviction that there was "no hope without dope", psychedelic drugs didn't deliver the cognitive revolution their devotees hoped. Brand says it was Aldous Huxley's *The Doors of Perception* that first switched him on to the mind-expanding potential of psychedelic drugs: "At Stanford I encountered Aldous Huxley. And right after I got out of the army I was taking mescaline with artists outside of New York City and having amazing experiences. The line was 'No hope without dope'. This was going to be the great revelatory breakthrough for humankind. And it was for a while but then it tapered off pretty badly. It was nowhere near as radical as what computers have done. So I just, you know, shifted my allegiance in a sense from a semi-failed technology to a highly successful technology."

Despite the war on drugs, despite the constantly reconstituting government drug advisory panels and moral panics over designer drugs with implausible names, these days drugs like acid, ecstasy, dope and speed are classified as "recreational", with all the easy hedonism that nomenclature implies. So it's important to remember that psychedelics were once invested with the hopes of a generation as a serious, mind-expanding, "technology". In 1968, Brand had been one of over 150 test subjects detailed in the first-ever published research into the effects of LSD produced by the International Foundation for Advanced Study (IFAS), Myron Stolaroff's Menlo Park-based research centre. But it was a different kind of research that was going on in sixties West Coast America that ultimately turned Brand's head.

"The difference between drugs and computers," Brand tells me, "was that drugs levelled off and computers didn't. I mean, technology is supposed to come in S-curves. They develop gradually and then they get steep and then they level off. Computer technology has not done that yet. It just keeps going and enhances capability decade after decade. So putting that kind of a positive feedback at the heart of the human process of communication and calculation and the rest of it, is pretty damn fundamental stuff and it is the kind of revolution that we thought psychedelic drugs was going to be."

Brand is talking about "Moore's Law", a now long-term trend in computer hardware that means computer processing power doubles roughly every two years. Moore's Law was first identified by Intel co-founder Gordon E. Moore in 1965, who thought at the time that the trend was likely to continue until the min-1970s.

In fact, Moore's law is now expected to hold true until at least 2015.

Douglas Engelbart, an electrical engineer who would later catch Brand's attention, had intuitively understood Moore's Law many years before it had been put into words, and in the late fifties and early sixties had set about designing the prototypes for components of the personal computers Engelbart was sure would result from this massive scaling of computer power. It was Brand's encounters with Engelbart that switched him on to the cognitive potential of an alternate technology to psychedelics. "Basically," Brand continues, "I was just being in the Bay area paying attention to interesting people. So for the same reason I was paying attention to Ken Kesey, I was paying attention to Doug Engelbart."

In December 1968, Engelbart demonstrated a number of his experimental ideas to a conference of computer scientists in the San Francisco Convention Center. The event was later dubbed "The Mother of all Demos", thanks to the fact that it was the world's first sighting of a number of computing technologies, including the mouse, email and hypertext. According to Steven Levy, author of *Hackers: Heroes of the Computer Revolution*, "Engelbart's support staff was as elaborate as one would find at a modern Grateful Dead concert" and that support staff included Stewart Brand, who volunteered a lot of time to set up the networked video links and cameras that made Engelbart's demonstration go off with such a bang.

Today, you can watch the 100-minute demonstration online, on the Stanford University website. Engelbart's voice echoes across the fuzz of the broadcast audio, giving him an Orson Welles quality which is only augmented by the vision of his disembodied head, cradled in a headset and microphone, fading in and out of the main camera shot which is pointed directly at the computer screen he has projected in front of the audience. Shots too, of his team, including Brand, stationed live at Menlo Park, orchestrating parts of the demonstration, fade in and out. Because it's the sixties, the whole film has a sci-fi quality to it, a feeling which must have been shared by the audience at the time, but for opposite reasons. On occasion, the film shows only a flat blinking cursor, awaiting commands while a second green-on-black dot flits around the screen, controlled by Engelbart's mechanical mouse, which he directs with his right hand. Thus Engelbart methodically demonstrates his cut-and-paste text editing, his hyperlinking, and his hierarchical file systems. The historic demonstration is celebrated among computer engineers to this day.

What inspired Douglas Engelbart's genius was as far away from the hippy culture in which Brand was ensconced as it is possible to get. In 1945, about a month before Little Boy dropped on Hiroshima, Vannevar Bush – the primary organiser of the Manhattan Project – published an essay in *Atlantic Monthly* called "As We May Think". At the time, Bush was working as the chief administrator of the application of science to warfare: as Director of the Office of Scientific Research and Development, he coordinated the activities of some 6,000 scientists. The essay was republished, in an abridged form, a month after the atom bomb dropped. It is widely interpreted as sketching a path for new collaborations of scientists from different disciplines in peacetime. But it is most notable for the general-purpose information storage and retrieval machine it proposes, the "memex".

According to John Markoff, author of *What the Dormouse Said: How the Sixties Counter-culture Shaped the Personal Computer Industry*, at around about the time America's nuclear bomb destroyed the city of Hiroshima – killing 80,000 of its residents, maiming tens of thousands more, and ending Japan's involvement in World War II – Doug Engelbart was sailing out of San Francisco harbour on his way to do his military service in the Philippines. He and his co-passengers even saw the VJ

Day celebrations beginning on the shore as they sailed away. It was in the Philippines that Engelbart marked time in a grass hut that had been converted into a library. And it was in this library that he read "As We May Think", and decided to make Bush's memex a reality.

Reading "As We May Think" today brings home just how far the development of personal computer technology travelled in the course of the second half of the twentieth century. In 1945, the US's leading scientist still needed to describe how each of the different mechanical disciplines – image capture, typewriting, microfiche – might need to develop in order to eventually combine, and create the "memex". Today, we are so at home with the general-purpose machine – the computer – that the memex that presaged it sounds like a phantasmagoria of dying technologies strapped together for survival. Bush describes his vision:

> Photocells capable of seeing things in a physical sense, advanced photography which can record what is seen or even what is not, thermionic tubes capable of controlling potent forces... cathode ray tubes...

In fact, the memex reminds me of the disembodied Heath Robinson creations I saw littering the floor in the basement at the Chaos Communication Congress. But outside of Chaos, your average 21st-century computer user will be more familiar with the computer components that Doug Engelbart troubled himself over than with anything Vannevar Bush wrote about. Ask a child to draw a computer and he will draw a keyboard, screen, mouse and – possibly – a box sitting next to it. Yet the box *is* the computer – the rest of it is just input and output devices.

Engelbart was not an acid head, but according to John Markoff he, like Brand, had taken part in the IFAS experiments, with mixed results. His first dose of LSD left the reclusive engineer catatonic. In a later experiment, a weaker, second dose was administered before participants, including Engelbart, were asked to work on a selection of engineering problems. According to Markoff:

> Engelbart's contribution to the creativity session was a toy he conceived... called... a "tinkle toy", and it was a little waterwheel that would float in a toilet bowl and spin when water (or urine) was run over it. It would serve as a potty training teaching aid for a little boy, offering him an incentive to pee in the toilet.

Today we might be just as inspired by Engelbart's "tinkle toy" as we are by his computer mouse. But that's only because the mouse, unlike the tinkle toy, has become so ubiquitous. Back in the sixties when Engelbart came up with the idea, the problem of how to point at something on a screen such that a computer could interpret what was being pointed at was one of the most pressing and difficult human/machine interaction problems faced by engineers.

Indeed, the very idea that machines and man could work in tandem (so-called "cybernetics") was a tenuous one, but it was one that sent Brand's senses reeling. If drugs weren't going to expand man's mind, perhaps computers could. Brand quickly set about proclaiming the good news.

In 1968, Brand and his wife Lois fired up their Dodge pickup and set about touring the hippy communes of America. This was the "Whole Earth Truck Store", and the Dodge acted as an alternative lending library, spreading word about access to tools and whole systems thinking, including cybernetics. The "Whole Earth" in this and Brand's later projects, had its roots in an acid trip two years earlier, when Brand had been sat on a rooftop, looking up to the stars, and asked himself "Why haven't we seen a picture of the whole earth yet?" (a question that, according to Tom Wolfe, he would later reproduce on pin badges and sell for 25¢ apiece).

Brand believed that such an image had the potential to both unite mankind, and to foster a new respect for the planet's environmental systems. At about the same time, James Lovelock was engaged in similar thinking, thinking that would eventually lead him to formulate his famous Gaia Theory. For Brand, and for the hippies who bought into his "Whole Earth" enthusiasm, the idea of the earth as a system was a powerful one. And it was also seductive: it certainly looked like a better system than the military industrial complex they had fled back to the land from.

Later in 1968, back in Menlo Park, Brand began preparations for the first print run of the "Whole Earth Catalog", a Sears catalogue for hippy communards that juxtaposed practical advice and tools for back-to-the-landers with intellectual stimulation in the form of reviews of books Brand and his fellow editors thought should be informing the ideals of their peers. The first edition ran to 66 pages, and was published in the autumn. Books on yoga practice and female sensuality sat next to ads for meditation cushions and sturdy, outdoor boots. One page carried the design for an Indian tipi, alongside a review of the book it was taken from. Knitting wools, manuals for sculptors and glass-blowers were all advertised, as well as books about Kibbutzim, and land sale catalogues.

The outsized volume was divided into several sections: "Whole Earth Systems" stood out at the front, followed by "Shelter and Land Use", "Industry and Craft", "Communications", "Community", "Nomadics" and "Learning". Interspersed throughout the catalogue, but particularly in the front section, lie texts about computer science, informatics, brain research and cybernetics. A two-page spread is given over to the works of Buckminster Fuller. The September 1966 edition of *Scientific American*, subtitled simply "Information", is touted as "the best introduction we've seen to computer science". Opposite it sits a gushing review of the HP 9100A Calculator, "the best of the new tabletop number-crunchers". On the previous page sits a review of *The Human Biocomputer,* an exploration into psychedelics and sensory deprivation by the neuroscientist John Lily, inventor of the flotation tank. The page following it features the McGraw-Hill encyclopaedia of Space.

Sitting respectably on page 12, Norbert Wiener's now seminal work on cybernetics, *The Human Use of Human Beings* is described as "social, untechnical, ultimate in most of its consideration. Its domain is the whole earth of mind." Later in the catalogue, Wiener's other great work, *Cybernetics, or Control and Communication in the Animal and the Machine* is reviewed. Wiener is described by the reviewer – presumably

Brand – as "one of the founders of an n-dimensional world whose nature we've yet to learn. He is also one of the all-time nice men."

In a talk he gave in 2005, Apple CEO Steve Jobs called the *Whole Earth Catalog* "one of the bibles of my generation", describing it as a Google in paperback form, idealistic and overflowing with incredible tools. *Wired* founder Kevin Kelly compared it to the modern-day blogosphere, calling it "a great example of user-generated content" thanks to Brand's habit of encouraging readers to submit their own reviews and earn themselves a fee of $10. It won a National Book Award – the first, and probably only time, a catalogue ever won such a plaudit.

The *Whole Earth Catalog* came out about a dozen times in full editions and updates between 1968 and 1972. Although the Whole Earth franchise persists today, the "end" of the Whole Earth Catalog happened in June 1971 when Stewart Brand threw a "demise" party at the Exploratorium Museum in San Francsico. Here's Brand in 1974, writing about the party:

> The Exploratorium staff had their museum weirding around us at full steam... And then at midnight Scott Beach announced from the stage that these here two hundred $100 dollar bills... were now the property of the party-goers. Just as soon as they could decide what to do with them.

The money was the proceeds of the Whole Earth Catalog. And the guests, unsurprisingly, had a hard time deciding how to invest it:

> The debate lasted till 9 a.m. the next morning, when a dozen remaining hardcore turned the remaining $15,000 ($5,000 had been distributed to the crowd at one wild point) over to Fred Moore, dishwasher.

But Fred Moore wasn't just a dishwasher. Not only was he a veteran of the early non-violent protest movement, now he was into the promise of personal computers in a big way. Most of the money Moore received the night of Stewart Brand's Demise Party eventually went into founding the Homebrew Computer Club, a place for amateur and professional computer enthusiasts to tinker with personal computers.

And so from the ashes of the *Catalog* rose a legendary phoenix. For it was at Homebrew that Steve Wozniak would meet Steve Jobs, and the two decide to found Apple Computers. Lee Felsenstein, designer of the first mass-produced portable computer the Osborne 1, also hung out there, as did the legendary telephone network hacker or "phreak" John "Captain Crunch" Draper. And it was to the Homebrew Computer Club that a 20-year old Bill Gates wrote his disgruntled "Open letter to Hobbyists".

After the *Catalog's* demise party, Brand reached out to a wider audience. Writing for *Rolling Stone* magazine in 1972, Brand announced

> Ready or not, computers are coming to the people. That's good news, maybe the best since psychedelics.

The article was about *Space War* (subtitled "Fanatic Life and Symbolic Death Among the Computer Bums"), a computer game Brand had witnessed young engineers playing at the Stanford Computation Center.

Four decades later, back in our comfy hotel lounge, he relates the scene to me: "What I saw was the back room of this computation centre, and a bunch of young computer programmers playing *Space War*, which was the first what we would call video game. And they were in a state of ecstasy, as near as I could tell. I mean they were mashing these buttons and operating, just a toggle that moved their rocket ships around on the PDP11 screen, which was one of the first of the mini-computers. And five of them playing simultaneously and enthusiastic beyond any out of body experience I'd ever seen."

Brand had a sense that profound things were going on, "and I've sort of been drumming my fingers ever since because so many of the things that were foreseen at that point took a long time to arrive. So when I did the piece for *Rolling Stone* (the magazine's publisher) Jann Wenner said at the time, 'Well, you've just set in motion a whole new body of journalism that's going to track down all this stuff.' And in fact, it was ten years later that Steven Levy did the book *Hackers*, which sort of told the rest of the story."

Spurred on by Levy's *Hackers*, in 1984, the same year of the inaugural Chaos Communication Congress in Germany, Brand convened the US's first Hacker Con, in Marin County, California. "Organising the Hackers' Conference was like some of the early hacking at MIT, so collaborative and rapid you couldn't keep track of who did what..." he wrote at the time, "But once they were on the scene, they were the world's easiest group to work with. If anything went wrong 1) they didn't care, 2) they could fix it." In the end, Brand attracted around 125 hackers to the upmarket camping resort, providing tools, a place to sleep and "enough candy and soda to get them through the night". Twenty computer reporters were also invited and a film of the event, *Hackers: Wizards of the Electronic Age* was broadcast on PBS and is available to watch on YouTube today.

By now – in the middle of the Western world's headiest decade – the interface problems that had kept Engelbart occupied were solved, and the personal computer world was surfing high on Moore's law's ever-rising wave. A new breed of hackers was working on code, with commercial as well as personal success. The men (mostly - Brand records four women at the event) who gathered at Marin County were a mix of the original Homebrew crowd, computer engineers from MIT, Stanford and Xerox Parc, as well as a new breed of software coder, many of whom had already netted small personal fortunes from the 8-bit pinball arcade games and paint programs they'd designed and distributed. Because software code, like music and movies, attracts a copyright, many of the coders were receiving their earnings like rock stars, in the form of monthly or annual royalty cheques. Robert Woodhead, designer of roleplaying game *Wizardry* tells the camera "I never intended to make money, it just sort of hit me in the face". Bill Budge, creator of *Raster Blaster* computer pinball remembers his first royalty cheque: "And I was just blown away. This was more money than I wanted to sell [exclusive rights to the games for]. One month's royalties."

Needless to say, rich or not, most of these guys look a universe away from the eighties rockstar aesthetic: one particular Mac hacker, Andy Hertzfelt, who the documentary reveals has just sold a coded user interface feature to Apple for $100,000, wears a jumper whose collar frays dangerously apart from the sleeve, threatening to detach one arm completely and send a cascade of cheap polycotton down his mouse-operating arm.

The *Hackers...* documentary focuses on the discord among the hackers over whether the new money coming in is a good thing. A TV voiceover in the scholastic style informs us:

> Philosophical hackers and early phone phreaks believe that information and tools should be free... and they openly share their work with others. Today, hackers are divided between the old values and the new.

It's clear from film of the discussion that many from the original academic and Homebrew communities believe that computers could never have got where they have without hackers freely sharing the code that would make them work. Back in the days of time-share computers, when computer time was limited and every second with the machine counted, coders, be they hobbyists or professors, would routinely leave the tapes that operated computer programs in the drawer next to the workstation, for the next guy to use and build on.

Could computer code continue to be shared in this way? Some of the newer coders, much like musicians or painters, express their sense that this would impinge on their artistic rights, that the code they ship is the finished product, and any hacker add-ons an insult to their creative vision. Others protest that without sharing code, the development of the computer will stagnate, and the freedom of a hacker to do what he loves best – hack – will be impinged upon. And then there is the question of how to make money. Although a number of hackers detail how they are still making a good living despite sharing their code with other hackers, everyone agrees those royalty cheques will get smaller if code was routinely given away for free.

Enter a 31-year-old Richard Stallman, captioned by the filmmakers as "MIT's last hacker", because, they say, of his decision to remain at the scholarly Massachusetts Institute of Technology despite the temptations of the commercial world. "My project is to make all software free," he announces at the beginning of the film in a high-pitched, nasal, New York accent. Later on, he describes for the filmmakers his objections to code that is not shared:

> Imagine if you bought a house, and the basement was locked, and only the original building contractor had the key. If you needed to make any change, repair anything, you had to go to him. And if he was too busy doing something else he'd tell you to get lost and you'd be stuck... You're at that person's mercy, and you become downtrodden and resigned. That's what happens when the blueprints to a computer program are kept secret by the organisation that sells it, and that's the usual way things are done.

"Free as in freedom", then, not "free as in beer" – Stallman might perhaps have felt more at home among the public-spirited hackers at the 1984 Chaos Communication Congress than amongst Brand's happy hippy millionaires. By the time he had arrived at Marin County, Richard Stallman was less than a year into a project that would significantly shape the next twenty, and not just in the world of computing. That project was the GNU operating system, and Stallman's ambition was to create a complete computer software package that could be shared and modified freely by its users in perpetuity. By reverse engineering the copyright system that was making millionaires of his fellow Marin County hackers, Stallman created "copyleft", a watertight legal safeguard against digital enclosure that basically says, "here, you can take a copy of this, but only if you always share what you do with it with other people like I shared this with you". Coupled with the millions of man-hours that have since gone in to coding GNU (now known as GNU/Linux, or – to Stallman's rightful ire – simply "Linux") copyleft is one of the main reasons today's worldwide web is as interesting as it is.

A quarter of a century later, I'm not sure we'd care what Andy Hertzfelt, Robert Woodhead or Bill Budge had to say if it weren't for Richard Stallman. His free software project effectively sewed a piece of the MIT hacker past into the worldwide web future, ensuring there was always a section of the global software codebase that could be developed and shared by anyone who cared enough to fire up a command line. Without him, the world of computers might still be 8-bit parlour games and Microsoft Paint. And there isn't much revolutionary in that.

Today, the GNU/Linux operating system runs on more than half of the computers that serve the World Wide Web, and all the many hundreds of thousands of computers that run Google's search engine. Early on in my career as a tech journalist, I met Richard Stallman at a meeting of free software enthusiasts held in the Postal Workers Union in Edinburgh. By that time, some 20 years into the GNU project, his New York trill had mellowed, but his vision of free software was just as clear. At first I didn't realise why Stallman was constantly rubbing baby oil in his hands; it was only later I understood he is often troubled by a repetitive strain injury from this obsessive coding in the eighties and nineties, and has been unable to seriously code anything for some time. Richard Stallman coded most of the first versions of GNU all by himself.

Speaking to camera, and with only slightly more hair than he has today, Stewart Brand explains how he sees the hackers at Marin County:

> They are shy, sweet, incredibly brilliant, and I think more effective in pushing the culture around now in good ways than almost any group I can think of.

Later, in a report in the *Catalog* spin-off the *Whole Earth Review* he would call them "the most interesting and effective body of intellectuals since the framers of the US constitution".

In this report there's also a transcript of some of conversations that took place in Marin County away from the cameras. The talk about code freedom still clearly dominates. At one point Brand mediates proceedings with the following statement:

> On the one hand information wants to be expensive, because it's so valuable. The right information in the right place just changes your life. On the other hand, information wants to be free, because the cost of getting it out

> is getting lower and lower all the time. So you have these two fighting against each other.

It's a prescient observation, one that captures a whole heap of preoccupations that we suffer from a quarter of a century later – from the importance of privacy in the digital age to how Rupert Murdoch proposes to sell newspapers over the web. But, perhaps unfortunately, Brand's words made it into posterity in a highly abridged form:

> "Information wants to be free."

One development that has done more to free information than perhaps even the personal computer, is only mentioned in passing in the *Hackers* documentary. The narrator informs us:

> Another channel for the free exchange of information is now available on various computer networks and electronic bulletin boards nationwide. By dialling these systems through a simple phone hook up called a modem, users can send and receive messages in seconds and chat with others thousands of miles away.

This, then, is the internet. If the man/machine synergy of personal computing was to replace psychedelic drugs as the true path to cognitive enhancement for those in the counterculture still sober enough to grasp it, then the computing world also had its own version of the hippy commune up its sleeve. Because although Brand had made a small fortune out of the hippies back when he was selling the *Catalog* around the communes of West America, the fortunes of the communes themselves had been less positive.

Brand sounds circumspect as he talks to me about the ultimate failure of commune living: "My generation is lucky in that we all got to go out and try to make communes work, which pretty much universally failed for various reasons." For me, the reason for the failure of the hippy commune is perfectly captured in another scene from *Easy Rider*.

Captain America and Billy have just arrived at a commune, brought there by a strange man they've picked up on the road. The man goes over to greet a woman, who is standing in the communal kitchen looking worn out and pissed off. As Dennis Hopper's camera pans around a scene of rural idyll – children running naked, chickens, artists – the woman's voice is foregrounded. We don't see her face as she talks, so we miss out on her hippy paraphernalia (long hair, low-cut, flowing dress). Her voice is sharp, it could belong to any mid-American housewife: "We can't take any more strangers... Last week, Susan dropped in with people from Easter City. She wanted to take pounds of rice with her. Naturally, we had to say no. So she gets uptight, breaks out some hash and won't give us any."

Says Brand: "We thought that our ideas would prevail. And ideas don't prevail in social situations. I mean, people sign the contract and then realise it sucks and then they leave."

A year after Marin County, Brand founded the Whole Earth 'Lectronic Link (The WELL), one of the earliest and most influential online communities. This was 1985, the cutting edge technology of the time was the bulletin board system (BBS), electronic community notice boards members could access by dialling in through a phone line using a modem to connect them via their personal computer. The WELL was one such system, and to cover its costs it charged its members a subscription fee.

As a WELL member, your fee got you access to a selection of "conferences" – discussions that reflected member interests in anything from arts and media to software and business. As the technology developed and the network that connected academic institutions began to accept commercial traffic, the WELL became one of the first internet service providers.

The early WELL moderators included Matthew McClure and Cliff Figallo both of whom had lived in The Farm, a religious commune in Tennessee. The WELL quickly became known as the online hangout of Deadheads, the dedicated fans of the Merry Pranksters' in-house band, the Grateful Dead. And so it was that the sixties vibe was preserved into the eighties and beyond, if only on disk, in an imagined collective space each member could enjoy from the comfort of their own private home.

"If the 'net has an online equivalent of the Algonquin Round Table, the WELL might be it," writes journalist Wendy Grossman in her 1997 book, *net.wars*. The WELL inspired a number of enterprises that are household names today, including Craigslist, the free classified ads service that is gradually hollowing out the local newspaper industry, and *Wired* magazine.

The WELL also provided the backdrop for one of the earliest confrontations between Brand's generation of sixties Utopians and the harder-edged ideologies of a new generation set to marshal the 'net into the 21st century. In 1990 (the year of the first networked computer virus), the WELL was *Harpers* magazine's cyberspatial venue of choice when it decided to investigate the darker side of computer hacking by inviting New York-based crackers including Phiber Optik and Acid Phreak to join the techno-hippies for an online debate. John Perry Barlow, former lyricist of the Grateful Dead and now the unofficial scribe of the WELL community, documented the experience in his essay *Crime And Puzzlement*:

> These kids were fractious, vulgar, immature, amoral, insulting, and too damned good at their work. Worse, they inducted a number of former kids like myself into Middle Age. The long feared day had finally come when some gunsel would yank my beard and call me, too accurately, an old fart.

Despite what Barlow called "a steady barrage of typed testosterone", including one incident where Phiber Optik uploaded a hacked copy of Barlow's entire credit history to prove a point, the Grateful Dead man was compelled to learn more about this representative of a new generation of "cyberpunks", and arranged to meet him offline – first over the phone, and then in person. What he discovered behind the bravado was "an intelligent, civilized, and surprisingly principled kid of 18 [whose] cracking impulses seemed purely exploratory". "I've begun to wonder," he continues, "If we wouldn't also regard spelunkers as desperate criminals if AT&T owned all the caves."

The experience left Barlow worried for his new friends, and for the reaction their activities might provoke from law-enforcing authorities:

> Their other favorite risky business is the time-honored adolescent sport of trespassing. They insist on going where they don't belong. But then teen-age boys have been proceeding uninvited since the dawn of human puberty... I broke into NORAD when I was 17. A friend and I... tried to get inside the Cheyenne Mountain. The chrome-helmeted Air Force MPs held us for about two hours before letting us go. They weren't much older than us and knew exactly our level of national security threat. Had we come cloaked in electronic mystery, their alert status certainly would have been higher.

Bureaucracies, Barlow argues in *Crime and Puzzlement*, will naturally over-react to poorly-understood "cyber-threats", and in trying to do the job of parents regulating the behaviour of childish online trespassers, will crush the new-found freedom of the online sphere for the grown-ups, too. It was these experiences which contributed to Barlow's decision to found the Electronic Frontier Foundation, the world's first digital civil liberties organisation, along with EFF co-founders Mitch Kapor and John Gilmore. The EFF initially took on legal cases of hackers targeted by the FBI's two-year crackdown on computer-related activities, *Operation Sundevil*, as well as academic researchers and entrepreneurs whose work attracted the attention of the authorities. But although so-called "impact litigation" remains a central part of the its operations to this day, as legislators began to ponder how to regulate the 'net, the EFF's work quickly stretched beyond the courtroom and into the corridors of Washington DC.

It was in reaction to the US government's Telecommunications Act of 1996, which he labelled an "atrocity [that would] place more restrictive constraints on the conversation in Cyberspace than presently exist in the Senate cafeteria", that John Perry Barlow penned his most famous work, the *Declaration of the Independence of Cyberspace.* The text, which continues to be extensively cited by those wishing to capture the early libertarian idealism of the 'net, begins:

> Governments of the Industrial World, you weary giants of flesh and steel, I come from Cyberspace, the new home of Mind. On behalf of the future, I ask you of the past to leave us alone. You are not welcome among us. You have no sovereignty where we gather.

Although this story – the story of how a bunch of sixties hippies got tired of tripping and uploaded themselves to a new electronic frontier – is not unknown, I'm always surprised it's not better known. After all, it's not just me who's obsessed with hippy counterculture and where it disappeared to. Thanks to a mainstream media made up of aging baby-boomers, nostalgia for the swinging sixties permeates contemporary culture to an asphyxiating degree. And our obsession with new technology and the power of the web is almost as intense.

I took a long time to get it, too. I was into web culture and free software, had heard the mantra "information wants to be free", and had even believed it, way before I joined the dots between my obsession with *Easy Rider* and my love of all things cyberspace. It wasn't until a copy of Fred Turner's book *From Counterculture to Cyberculture* landed on my desk at a magazine I was working at in 2006 that the world of the WELL, the Homebrew Computer Club and the Whole Earth Catalog opened up for me. And when it did, I wasn't entirely pleased. I had thought the web was where the children of the baby boomers got to have their own space, to play with their own ideas, away from the complex political legacy of gender equality and identity politics, of the cult of the individual and the advance of corporate "freedom". But it turned out all we were doing was gardening in someone else's Utopia.

I ask Stewart if he would describe himself these days as a techno-Utopian.

"The very concept of techno-Utopian", he replies, "would be part of what we trend against. Because techno-Utopia says *Brave New World*. We, the technoids, know the future and are spelling it out for you. That's what Utopia is. It's there in Plato and it's there in Thomas More.

"Utopias in practice are invariably Dystopias. So Utopia tells you that Dystopia will happen when you try to plan ahead."

In the final paragraphs of his declaration, John Perry Barlow's defies the ability of states to regulate the 'net, and sets out his belief in the virtual Utopia which is to come:

> In the United States, you have today created a law, the Telecommunications Reform Act, which repudiates your own Constitution and insults the dreams of Jef-

> ferson, Washington, Mill, Madison, DeToqueville, and Brandeis. These dreams must now be born anew in us... These increasingly hostile and colonial measures place us in the same position as those previous lovers of freedom and self-determination who had to reject the authorities of distant, uninformed powers. We must declare our virtual selves immune to your sovereignty, even as we continue to consent to your rule over our bodies. We will spread ourselves across the Planet so that no-one can arrest our thoughts.
>
> We will create a civilization of the Mind in Cyberspace. May it be more humane and fair than the world your governments have made before.

"Information wants to be free"; "We will create a civilisation of Mind": whether or not they stand by their words today, it is these two idealists, Barlow and Brand, who first articulated the philosophy of freedom through networked, digital technology that was to drive the next generation of hackers and geeks. As the rest of the world woke up to the web, it was up to this next generation to explain and, eventually, and defend those ideals. And it wasn't going to be easy.

chapter

just kids

Chapter 4: Just Kids

I hear from Rop Gonggrijp again in late January, a week after my meeting with Brand. I'm logged into Skype when he pops up in my chat window to let me know he's in Reykjavik, working with Julian Assange from WikiLeaks.

"Working on the revolution here," he types, before sending me a link to the planned "Media Freedom Bill" he hopes Iceland's Parliament will vote to adopt soon. I glance at it – it looks interesting. A message flashes on my screen: "Wanna help?"

The thing is, I'm not sure if I do. But Rop doesn't stay online to hear my answer.

Later that week, I'm sitting in the Clerkenwell offices of Cory Doctorow, holding a solid gold coin worth around £1,000. It's the Prometheus Award, bestowed on Cory in 2009 by the Libertarian Futurist Society. "It's the most valuable award given in science fiction," Doctorow explains, "They give you gold in case society collapses."

Sat on a red leather chair in Doctorow's offices in Clerkenwell, I'm faced by shelving running wall-to-wall-to-ten-foot-high-ceiling, neatly stacked with the books and ephemera that define this man's public profile. Cory is not just a science fiction writer. In fact, he's one of the most vocal digital civil rights campaigners on the web today, a former outreach officer for the Electronic Frontier Foundation, and (when he came to the UK several years ago to get married and start a family) a founder of the Open Rights Group. He is also one of the world's most prolific bloggers, co-editor of BoingBoing.net, on and off the most popular blog on the web, and read by millions of people worldwide.

On the shelves in front of me, graphic novels and books on futurism regularly give way to Victoriana, skulls, self-portraits and artfully mutated kids' toys. Hung on the wall is an old Swiss cuckoo clock (Cory's birthday present this year from his wife, gamesblogger and now Channel 4 executive, Alice Taylor), which makes itself known at half-hour intervals during the length of our interview. The scene is exactly as you would expect if you had followed BoingBoing.net for any length of time. When I was first getting into geek culture, BoingBoing.net was my guide, and Cory Doctorow my hero. The first time I met him was at the 2004 Big Brother Awards ceremony, a tongue-in-cheek annual event run by Privacy International to name and shame people who do damage to privacy and civil rights (the winners, which that year included British Gas and the NHS IT programme, rarely show up to collect their honours). I had no idea what he looked like, but I guessed who he was from his punk leather jacket and vintage specs, not to mention his entourage. Cory manages to capture much of what is hip about being a geek, while remaining earnestly committed to hacker values. He is the perfect example of someone who took up Brand's vision of information abundance and made it his own.

Pointing to the gold coin, Cory explains, "It's probably the only thing burglable in this office when I close the door, and probably no-one would ever notice it". Doctorow won the Prometheus Award for *Little Brother,* a near-future adventure romp aimed at a young adult audience. In the novel, a bunch of West Coast teenagers overthrow a corrupt and brutal state through a combination of guts and tech stealth. "I'm up for the award again this year," says Cory. "The Libertarian Futurist Society are the nicest people and the last four years running they have given the award to Marxists or the children of Marxists. Marxists or the children of Marxists appear to be writing the most libertarian science fiction."

Cory, who describes himself as a "civil libertarian", is in the latter camp, growing up in the thick of seventies and eighties radical politics in Canada. His dad, an intellectual kid from a family of Eastern European refugees, had renounced Judaism in favour of Marxism at age 18 after he'd lost an argument – the first argument he'd ever lost – with a Trotskyist picket captain. Before long, Cory's dad was writing and selling Trotskyist newspapers for a living with a protest group in Toronto, which is where he met Cory's mother, a pro-choice activist involved in the women's movement.

Cory was primed early on for the activist's life he now leads. "My mum used to take me on pro-choice marches. When I was five they told me I was going to march at my aunt's wedding and asked me if I knew how to march. And I said: 'Well, of course I do.' And I mimed marching up and down carrying a placard, shouting: 'Not the Church and not the State. Women must control their fate.'" At 12, Cory was detained with his dad at a sit-in at the Litton plant, a weapons factory made famous later in the same year by Canada's own Baader Meinhof-style group, the Squamish Five, when they bombed the plant in a botched operation that led to several injuries.

Adolescence did little to suppress the activist credentials of this 12-year old radical poster-child. But although Cory identifies a potential split "between what my father saw as kind of my bourgeois punk anarchism and his more rigorous Marxist approach", his most memorable breakaway from the older generation came at the annual peace and social justice summer camp his parents sent him to, Grindstone.

Cory describes Grindstone as "his Rosebud". Bequeathed to the Quakers by the daughter of its original owner, the first Admiral of the Royal Canadian Navy, Grindstone Island became an experimental centre of non-violent civilian defence against the backdrop of the Vietnam War. In 1965, it had been the setting for the disastrous "Grindstone experiment", a role-playing game designed to test theories of non-violent resistance that in the end only served to highlight their inefficacy: the entire exercise was curtailed two days early after half the non-violent party were "killed" by a staged invading force.

It was the mid-eighties by the time a young Cory arrived at Grindstone Island, and it was there that Cory's techno-Utopianism was to crystallise. "There was a guy who was involved in gender politics and youth sex education, who was involved with our youth caucus. He was a writer, educator and so on, and I remember him sat in our big fireplace room one night with his laptop, with his face bathed in its light. And I remember sitting there and just having this moment where I thought: 'That's it. That's perfect. You go to a place like Grindstone where you're off the grid and you're with your comrades and your extended political family but you're also connected and you've got your tools with you and you can write.' To see this proper tool there really kind of blew my mind and I thought, 'Will I someday be able to sit in the hammock at Moonwatcher's Point with a laptop on my lap?' This just blew my mind. I just remember thinking that that would be Utopia, right? To have that, back to the land and high tech kind of in one place."

I'm about to segue into a question about Stewart Brand when Cory beats me to it, reaching up to the shelf behind him. "So I wanted to show you this before we go further. This is my collection of *Whole Earth Catalogs*. I stole them from the library at Grindstone. I rate these as some of the most important books ever published."

It's the first time I've seen original copies of the *Whole Earth Catalog*, and as the cuckoo clock tick-tocks in the background

I take my time carefully turning the yellowing, oversize pages. Something hits me, something that hadn't occurred to me before. The *Catalog* and Cory's blog, BoingBoing.net, have a lot in common. I put this to Cory.

"Absolutely. 100%. I didn't do it consciously but one day I opened up that thing and I went: 'Oh my God, these are BoingBoing's layouts. Totally."

BoingBoing.net's original tagline is "A Directory of Wonderful Things". A directory is like a catalogue. And the items and ideas BoingBoing.net lists have the same contrasting qualities of DIY culture, progressive politics, and high tech – instructions on how to build your own robot rub up against reports on bloggers arrested in repressive states and the latest news from nanotech research. But there is one thing that BoingBoing.net brings that has nothing to do with Whole Earth, and that is a strong sense of kitsch, that post-modern tonic used liberally by the children of baby boomers to get them through the day.

The reference to the *Whole Earth Catalog* may have been unconscious, but by the time Cory was in his late teens, he was sold on the cyberpunk politics that Brand, Barlow and the rest of them were putting out through the Whole Earth's new instantiation, the *Whole Earth Review*.

"My friend, Karl Levesque, who I first met at Grindstone, was running an anarchist book store and he would send me magazines that had been returned for credit. And one day he sent me the *Whole Earth Review* issue called 'Is the Body Obsolete?', with William Gibson's articles and Hans Moravec and all these other people making the connection between cyberculture and counterculture. I must have been 16. This was completely transformational literature for me. Totally changed the way I thought about things."

Techno-Utopianism wasn't the only legacy Cory took from Grindstone – he also got his first taste of the hypocrisy of the hippy generation. "The adults involved with Grindstone saw as part of their mission as being to create a second generation, and that's why they did the youth camps, the kids' camps," says Cory. And yet the older generation at Grindstone ended up betraying Cory and his friends. Over the years, a youth caucus of Grindstone summer camp graduates had formed, who ran their own summer programming and took part in the governance of the organisation that ran the island. Slowly, the organisation ran out of money, and it became clear that they couldn't afford to keep the island up. And so the island was sold, netting the Grindstone co-op around $280,000.

The youth caucus proposed taking the money to build another conference centre that could be run more sustainably. Their vision was to do what the peace and social justice activists from the Vietnam era had done with Grindstone, offering training for a new generation of non-violent activists. They had a plot of land, and an arrangement with a group of experienced activists. But when the youth caucus submitted their proposal to the Grindstone Co-op adults, it was met with a cold scepticism Cory finds hard to bear even now.

"Grindstone had been started by Quakers who ran everything on a consensus basis," says Cory, "But you can't incorporate a consensus organisation. The by-laws had to have a basis for overcoming deadlocks. And so we had one – it was a majority vote of shares – but we had never really used it before." It was this system that was used to decide the issue, and the youth caucus lost out. "It just flew in the face of the history of consensus," Cory laments.

Although the youth wing received some of the grant money, which kept them going for a few more years, they eventually petered out. Cory is less than circumspect. "We might have petered out anyway but that was a real kind of angry activist split in my life where I felt like these people, who had said to us: 'Our mission is to turn you into our successors and we recognise that young people have the capacity to do anything in the world,' had then said: 'Actually, that was just bullshit. Young people can't really do anything, you know. Young people are just kids. You guys are just kids.'"

Bound up in the lifted copies of the *Whole Earth Catalog*, Cory took his techno-Utopianism with him when he left Grindstone. But it didn't always go down well in eighties Canada. "Being a technology fan among lefties of that era means that you were kind of a pariah," he explains, "Techno-Utopianism was not widely understood and technology was seen as, well... I was out there protesting cruise missile guidance systems, but the internet came from [the US military research agency] DARPA."

Nonetheless, Cory spent his late teens and early twenties working with activists and other non-profit organisations, attempting to switch them on to the potential of the new networked communications space. Part of this work was distributing grants from the Grindstone Island sale, including one to Web Networks, Canada's first non-profit technology provider, to connect Cree Native Americans in rural Saskatchewan with indigenous people in Brazil and other parts of South America via a web forum where they could share tips on fighting land claims. He also spent a few months in Costa Rica with Youth Challenge International (YCI), helping to build a local school while talking to anyone who'd listen about the need for YCI to upgrade to new internet-based technology. "The people who go off to do these projects are really back-to-the-lander types and they were really intensely sceptical." He stayed involved with the organisation for three or four years thereafter "basically forcing them to do IT."

"We don't realise it," explains Cory, "but the main job of activist organisers prior to 1995 or so was stuffing envelopes and setting up phone trees and just letting other people know what was going on. Mailman and Apache basically took 95% of the heavy lifting off the shoulders of activists."

So, if the 'net had been mainstream in the sixties, would the radical movements of the sixties and seventies, the ones Cory's parents devoted their lives to, have got further than they did?

Cory is unsure. "One thing about those groups is that they were very schismatic. They invented the flame war. I wonder if the 'net would have actually accelerated some of those schisms. Because they flew apart, those things flew apart in part due to their own inertia."

For the cyberpunks Cory followed in the eighties, the internet wasn't just a communications tool. As John Perry Barlow recognised when he formed the Electronic Frontier Foundation, the 'net was a place, a free place, and that freedom needed to be defended. Many of the threats to that freedom were similar to the threats to freedom found in the offline world – censorship, surveillance, and the electronic violence perpetrated by early virus writers. But some of them seemed entirely new, and it was against one of these new threats that Cory eventually allied himself. And just like his dad, it took an argument he couldn't win to convert him.

"My ideas about copyright weren't Canadian or activist, they were artistic. Like many people who are breaking into the arts, I learned everything I knew about copyright from older artists whose folk understanding of copyright amounted to: 'The more copyright you give away, the worse you get screwed'. I understood copyright as a labour right for artists."

That was about to change. Through a small online business he'd founded, Cory had got to meet EFF lawyers Cindy Cohn and Fred von Lohmann, and they'd become friends. In 2000 Cindy, Fred and Cory flew from San Francisco to Hong Kong together to speak at a music industry event to discuss responses to digital technology.

Cory continues, "I basically argued with Fred for 15 hours in the sky about copyright. And for four days in Hong Kong we went around to all the markets and we just argued about copyright for the entire trip. Then later we came to London together and we did it again. And I kind of had a conversion experience. I came around to really understand copyright as a utilitarian thing, copyright's limitations as being good for artists. All of that stuff arose from these dialogues with Fred and Cindy."

The EFF was interested in how the internet was forcing copyright – a set of laws originally designed to mediate the activities of commercial publishers in their dealings with artists – into territory that was starting to affect ordinary citizens' free speech rights. Copyright had allowed Richard Stallman, through his "copyleft" hack, to reverse the enclosure of software code in the eighties. But the more traditional creative industries were beginning to see how the internet's ability to distribute, at zero cost, perfect digital copies of the hit movies and songs they were used to selling on pretty bits of plastic might undermine their future business. The copyright enforcement measures they were proposing applied printing press-era copyright regulation to the activity of regular, internet-using citizens in the digital age, as destructive as applying EU regulations for catering firms or cash-crop farmers to domestic kitchens and gardens.

What's more, because copyright naturally creates monopolies (whereas anyone has the right to sell cupcakes, open clothes boutiques, or try and cure cancer, only one publishing company has the right to say what happens to the Beatles back catalogue, and only one movie company has the right to make sequels to *Star Wars*), law-makers were increasingly becoming the targets of slick, professional lobbyists hired by global media conglomerates to extract more control over markets by pleading that the rise of new technology was threatening the "sanctity" of copyright.

For Cindy and Fred, this was a topsy-turvy, through-the-looking-glass world, "where lawyers could argue with a straight face that it should be lawful for there to be wholesale bans on entire classes of speech, for the good of society". Cory went to work for EFF in 2002, and stayed for four years, much of which time was spent at the headquarters of the UN's World Intellectual Property Organisation (WIPO) in Geneva, agitating for reform.

Cory's first job at Geneva was to step into negotiations over the Broadcast Treaty. Cory arrived five years into negotiations, and witnessed the national delegates held captive by lobbyists from rights-holder groups and incumbent broadcasters. The proposals on the table were startling: a completely new copyright, afforded to broadcasters in everything they transmitted over their networks. What was worse, some delegates had been persuaded to propose that a similar exclusive copyright be granted to so-called "webcasters", an arrangement that could have handed untold powers to, for example, YouTube, over material they had had no hand in creating. It would, the EFF said, have "changed the nature of the Internet as a communication medium". And nobody was there to speak up for the 'net.

I interviewed Cory at the time, and his bafflement at the way things were progressing was palpable. "It's a very different world working at WIPO," he told me. "The most egregious lies are being told about how the world works and nobody is sticking their hand up and saying 'that's not true'". Cory and his colleagues began live-blogging negotiating sessions, getting the news of what was happening out online and in front of the people the new laws might affect. That was not the way things were normally done at WIPO, and eyebrows were raised. As he told me: "They characterise that as an abuse of their hospitality because we're telling tales. But it's the UN, right? The idea that the UN proceeds in secret is the stuff of paranoid fantasy."

Gradually, Cory and his colleagues turned the negotiations around, and in June 2007, the Broadcast Treaty was suspended indefinitely. It was a wonderful example of international democracy working as it should, and it got even better. The involvement at WIPO of NGOs like EFF, as well as the rise in negotiating power of countries like India, Brazil and China, whose economies currently do not rely so heavily on the exploitation of intellectual property, has now partly shifted WIPO's focus. Its slogan has changed from "WIPO is responsible for the promotion of the protection of intellectual property throughout the world" to "WIPO is dedicated to developing a balanced and accessible international intellectual property system", a recognition that development goals in the Global South and the rigorous enforcement of monopoly knowledge-ownership rights that mainly reside in the Global North are not necessarily compatible.

As a writer of science fiction, Cory practices what he preaches. His debut novel *Down and Out in the Magic Kingdom* was the first ever to be published under a Creative Commons licence, a sort of "copyleft" for art that allows creators to give away some of the rights they enjoy under copyright. With *Down and Out...*, Cory gave away the sole right to distribute the electronic version of the book, meaning Cory's fans could share it online without penalty.

Cory has written that giving away ebooks gives him artistic, moral and commercial satisfaction. All of Cory's subsequent novels, including *Little Brother*, have been released electronically on similar terms. The *Little Brother* licence is even more permissive, allowing readers to, as they say in the business, "transform" his work, so long as they don't profit from it and so long as they share any derived works on the same terms as the original licence Cory used. Cory keeps track of as many of the derived works as possible on his personal site, craphound.com. They include school plays and short films made by American students, as well as translations into Persian and Burmese circulated free online by pro-democracy activists in Burma and Iran.

Far from hindering his commercial success, Cory argues that Creative Commons has actually helped it ("ebooks sell print books"), and he might well be right – *Little Brother* spent more than a month on the *New York Times* bestseller lists.

It's a great book, a near-perfect articulation of the hopes and fears of the new generation of politically hungry hackers and geeks that are the heirs to Brand's techno-Utopian legacy. As the adults of San Francisco cower before the increasing demands of a Department of Homeland Security emboldened by a devastating terrorist attack on the San Francisco Bay Bridge, it is left to their children to restore democracy. The novel's lead protagonist, Marcus, is apprehended by the authorities after he finds himself near the scene of the terrorist bombing, playing truant from high school with his buddies to complete the next chapter in an alternative reality game. What follows during his three days of interrogation is more or less torture at the hands of the state, as DHS officials try and ascertain what Marcus and his friends were doing at the scene. Eventually, he and two other teammates are released, on instructions not to tell anyone where they have been. But one teammate, Daryl, is kept behind.

The San Francisco they return to has turned overnight into a police state, with checkpoints everywhere and a climate of fear that ostensibly keeps the adult population subdued, convinced that "the world isn't the same place it was last week". Buoyed up by his determination to free his friend, Marcus sets up a teenage resistance to the new regime. He establishes an underground digital communications network, based on chipped Xboxes loaded with free software, organising flash mobs of teenage protest and culture-jamming the DHS surveillance systems in an attempt to hold a mirror to the rights abuses of the DHS for long enough to pierce the adults' assurance that the new regime is in their best interests.

Marcus's relationship with his father exists as a kind of Socratic dialogue on the ethical aspects of the surveillance society, woven through the book as Marcus becomes more and more embroiled with the Department of Homeland Security's total surveillance of San Francisco's citizens. Just like Cory's father, Marcus's dad was a radical in his youth. But by the time we get to the events of *Little Brother*, he's earning his keep and saving up for Marcus' college education by consulting to "third-wave dotcoms that are doing various things with archives" in Silicon Valley. Correspondingly, his values have softened. Here's one key speech of his from the book:

> The Bill of Rights was written before data-mining. The right to freedom of association is fine, but why shouldn't the cops be allowed to mine your social network to figure out if you're hanging out with gangbangers and terrorists?...Would you rather have privacy or terrorists?

The dialogue reflects a shift in Cory's own thinking, but in the opposite direction. As he's grown up he's had to confront some of his youthful beliefs about the power of technology to make the world more free. The year the Berlin Wall came down Cory was 17 and, as he writes in the prologue to *Little Brother*, "communications tools were being used to bring information – and revolution – to the farthest-flung corners of the largest authoritarian state the Earth had ever seen." But for the 17-year-olds of today, computers are no longer benign. "The seductive little boxes on their desks and in their pockets watch their every move, corral them in, systematically depriving them of those new freedoms I had enjoyed and made such good use of in my young adulthood."

"I have a specific dreaded horror," Cory explains, "Of kids looking at computers and going 'These things are just used by adults to spy on us. Fuck them.' And maybe, because kids often don't have a very nuanced understanding of how this works, they'll move entirely to these walled garden services like Facebook and so on, where they're just being spied on, where Facebook are just spying on them and selling them on to marketing creeps.

"I think if that comes to pass they won't even know it. They won't even realise that the potential of computers was perverted. They'll assume that that's what computers were for."

Cory left EFF in 2006, and now describes himself as an "itinerant campaigner". And although he still agitates for copyright reform, he now has another focus for his advocacy – digital surveillance and the database state. If, as Stewart Brand foresaw, information now wants to be free, then that information is not just limited to software code, or medical patents, or music or literature. It's also information about us, data that reveals the detail of our private lives, our medical history, what books we like to read and where we like to travel. The rise of networked digital technology has, in the hands of the state as well as in the hands of old media marketing corporations and new media megaliths like Google, made a mockery of a human being's right to privacy. Which is not good news, considering privacy is the close cousin of human dignity, in turn the foundation of every human right going. And for all the energy government has spent trying to protect the intellectual property of major media corporations from the challenges of new technology, it has expended remarkably little energy on protecting its citizens from the radical invasions of privacy threatened by the very same technology. In fact, in most cases, it has positively colluded in sanctioning these invasions.

It's clear that, for Cory, the future of technology hangs in the balance. On the one hand the information abundance first described by Brand could work in humanity's favour, spreading knowledge and information around the world, promoting and enriching global democracy. But on the other hand, if all the technology ends up doing is enhancing the ability of a few powerful state and corporate players to keep tabs on the rest of the population, then humanity is likely to lose out big time.

Would Cory be prepared to call odds on which is the more likely future?

He sighs. "To be an activist is to be an optimist and a pessimist. So I'm on the one hand optimistic that we can prevent that from coming to pass and on the other hand I'm pessimistic that it'll come to pass unless we do something about it. So my odds are basically I think 100% if we do something about it, we'll solve it and I think 100% if we abandon it, it will come to pass. So that's what I think. Otherwise I wouldn't be doing it, right?"

chapter 5

Chapter 5: Anarchists in the UK

It's mid-March when Rop gets in contact again. When I answer my mobile to hear Rop's soft Dutch drawl, I find myself wishing I'd let the call go to my messages. I don't have any answers for Rop today. But that's not good enough, because he needs some.

"We need you in Reykjavik, can you come tonight?"

I um and ah, and after a while it's clear to both of us that I'm not up for it. I use work as an excuse, but I know what's holding me back is something different, something not dissimilar to fear. Rop is disappointed, but he tries not to let it show. I leave promising to help him find newspapers who might pay for advance use of WikiLeaks' next story, nurturing only a modest level of curiosity over what that might be.

A fortnight later Rop and Julian appear across the Atlantic at the National Press Club in Washington DC, to launch a video, *Collateral Murder*, made up of leaked US army footage which clearly shows their soldiers shooting two unarmed Reuters journalists in Iraq. The release makes headline news across the world.

I gave up being an activist after only two years trying. Partly this is because I'm not the kind of person who can survive without downtime, and to be a good activist you have to be committed to the cause every waking hour, and a few sleeping ones too. But I'm also not very good at playing games.

When I worked for the Open Rights Group, I spent a lot of my time at meetings in Westminster designed, I thought, to work out ways government could respond in the interests of citizens to problems posed by new technology. But despite the fact that this was already a fairly complicated thing to try and achieve, it soon became clear to me that the methods that had evolved for achieving it made it ten times more complicated – that is, nearly impossible. It's a tricky thing to describe, but spending any time at Westminster (or, even worse, Brussels) is like watching a group of people trying to decide how to direct rush hour traffic by playing an arcane version of cricket.

It's what people call politics, I suppose. For me, it was like eating a bad oyster. It left a taste in my mouth so foul I couldn't contemplate eating another one for a very long time.

The day after the release of *Collateral Murder*, on 6 April 2010, Gordon Brown calls the election. Although he has the option to dissolve Parliament immediately, instead he does what has become customary for British Prime Ministers since the early part of last century, and gives Parliament several days, ostensibly to tie up any legislative loose ends, a period known as "wash-up".

More than a third of the men and women still sitting in the House of Commons have less than a week left in their jobs. Collectively, they make up the most discredited Parliament in living memory. A year earlier, the *Daily Telegraph* published details of their expenses claims in a month-long exposé. It was damning information that their leader, the Speaker of the House of Commons Michael Martin, had sought to keep hidden for several years, using public money to appeal freedom of information decisions mandating publication up to the highest court of the land. What started out as a simple freedom of information request from an American journalist curious that such information wasn't already in the public domain, snowballed into the political scandal of the decade as it became clear that MPs had been using the expenses system as a politically expedient salary top-up scheme. That the scandal hit its peak just as the UK's public finances were descending into freefall only served to enrage the electorate more. Whatever mandate this band of brothers had, it was paper-thin.

While most of the country turned its mind to the forthcoming election campaigns and to who would make up the next Parliament, a small group of digital rights campaigners kept their attention on what this one had planned in its dying days. "Wash-up" is meant to be used for "non-controversial" legislation, intended to make sure that bills that are close to being passed, some of which may have had hundreds of man-hours of scrutiny and debate invested in them, are not lost in the cracks as overall power transfers from one Government to the next. But in our perverted democracy, wash-up long ago became the escape hatch for difficult policy – bills that legalised gambling and the building of super-casinos and bills that introduced the doomed National ID card scheme were both passed during previous pre-election wash-ups. Generally, what goes into wash-up is decided upon by the "whips", the wheeler-dealers of Parliament who use political party loyalty and the ultimate threat of party expulsion to get the results they want when it comes to a vote. Once a bill is in wash-up, it is generally passed without debate.

The bill we had our eyes on was the Digital Economy Bill, a complex piece of legislation covering everything from radio spectrum to broadband investment. Tucked into the bill were provisions that had the potential to mandate the mass disconnection of people from the internet if they had been accused of copyright infringement by rights-holding corporations. The provisions were both unworkable and utterly disproportionate – whole households could be disconnected based on the alleged infringement activity of one of its members, and the standards of proof required to make such an accusation were risible. Worse, instead of a proper legal process, the Digital Economy Bill invited corporations to monitor the online activity of millions of people, to interpret that activity as they saw fit, and then to act upon it, with all avenues of redress on behalf of the accused blocked by punitive legal expense.

After the EFF and other intellectual property reformers flushed the worst of the media lobbyists out of WIPO, those lobbyists didn't just go away. Although artists are beginning to see how the internet can bring them closer to their fans, augment their audiences, and yes, even increase their revenues through live appearances and nascent legal download and streaming services, these new models for rewarding creativity fairly online write traditional intermediaries like record labels out of the picture. They don't like that. The four major music companies – Warner, Universal, Sony-BMG and EMI – that together control over 75% of the global recorded music market have a lot to lose, and their response has been twofold. Firstly, they've blocked access to the back catalogues of all the Boomer favourites they control to anyone trying to invent new ways to legally and commercially access music online, either by flatly refusing to do business, or by charging exorbitant licence fees. And secondly, they've sought increasingly dark corners in which to speak to legislators and policymakers about enforcing copyright online, away from the sunlight of democratic scrutiny and proper debate. Disconnection provisions exactly like the ones being proposed by the Digital Economy Bill were turning up in all sorts of places – in proposals put forward by the European

Commission, but also in privileged, and secret, bilateral and multilateral trade negotiations across the world.

Given proper Parliamentary scrutiny, the Digital Economy Bill was unlikely to pass. Internet users across the UK were writing to their MPs, pointing out the flaws, and key consumer and industry bodies (like the hospitality industry, who argued that they would no longer be able to provide public wi-fi if they were held responsible for alleged infringements made by their customers) had made public statements condemning the disconnection provisions. "Wash-up" made all these problems go away. If the Digital Economy Bill was flawed, it didn't matter. It would get passed anyway, because that's how wash-up works.

The Open Rights Group organised a protest against the Digital Economy Bill outside of the Houses of Parliament. They came prepared with black, wordless placards and black gaffer tape to hand out to the roughly 100 protesters that attended, a visual indication of the dark days that lay ahead for online free expression. The result was certainly arresting, although given the profile of most of the protestors – young, long-haired boys and more than a handful of leather trench coats – it was also slightly menacing. A few MPs and prospective Parliamentary candidates appeared to show their support. I was there, too.

Cory Doctorow had been invited to rally the troops. As he took to the soapbox, he ripped the gaffer tape from his mouth, replacing it with a steam-punk looking copper megaphone (new protest rules around Parliament Square forbid, among other things, the use of amplified sound). He began to speak:

> So imagine if I said to you that I had a single wire that could deliver freedom of speech, freedom of the press, freedom of assembly, access to communities, ideas and tools, access to education, civic engagement, politics, everything that matters in the 21st century. And then I said we're going to take that wire and regulate it as though it were a glorified way of getting Lily Allen music and Police Academy sequels. You would say I was mad. But that's what's on the plate today with the Digital Economy Bill... The idea that we will disconnect entire households because one person who happens to live there has been accused - without any proof - of having done something naughty with copyright is so vastly disproportionate that it's amazing to hear that grown adults are actually contemplating it.

During a late evening session a few brave MPs opposed the whips and made eloquent attempts to argue against the bill to an empty chamber. But when the bell rang for the vote, the party faithful briefly left their drinks at the House of Commons bar and filed in dutifully to cast their passing votes. It was horrifying to watch these so-called elected representatives ignorant of the arguments and deaf to the complaints of their constituents – a record 50,000 people had written to or telephoned their MPs ahead of the vote, urging them to rebel. The Digital Economy Bill was now the Digital Economy Act. A month later we voted out the pack of bastards, but it didn't make me feel any better.

Rop IMs me several days after the Digital Economy Bill vote: "Did _you_ ever miss a party", he taunts.

I'm still distracted by the dismal performance of my own elected representatives to contemplate what I missed in Reykjavik. Rop is upbeat when I mention the Digital Economy Bill vote. "It's stuff like this that galvanizes a new generation's takeover," he assures me, "I sort of hope they go nuts with it. Disconnect families for downloading, the works. They need to find out what that unleashes sooner or later. And better there than over here..." I guess "here" means the Netherlands. I don't know where he is, but evidently he's not in the UK.

It's a week after the election, and I'm in a pub in Lewes with Phil Booth. Phil is the National Coordinator of NO2ID, the campaign against ID cards and the database state. At well over six-and-a-half foot tall, with shoulder-length hair and a broad Midlands accent, Phil cuts an imposing figure. It seems right that he should live here in Lewes, the historically subversive town in which, among other things, Thomas Paine enjoyed his political awakening.

Phil is a man I've been glad to have on my side over the years. When I first started working for the Open Rights Group, it was Phil who schooled me in the ways of Westminster, Phil who helped me navigate the perils of running a campaign based on popular funding and support. Once, at a drinks reception hosted by my old paper the *New Statesman* for the 2008 Labour Party conference in Manchester, Phil came to my rescue as I was being verbally abused by a drunk lobbyist for the record industry. Phil is not someone anyone would want to mess with.

Lewes' "Bonfire Boys" have a motto: "Our cause is just and must prevail". Every bonfire night, men in leather aprons built just like Phil roll burning barrels of tar up the high streets of Lewes or carry flaming crosses under this banner. The tradition started in the early 17th century, both to celebrate the uncovering of the Gunpowder Plot, and to commemorate the burning of 17 Protestant martyrs 50 years earlier outside Lewes' town hall. More like an organised riot than the family-friendly, fireworks-and-sparklers events hosted elsewhere in Britain, today Lewes Bonfire Night is the biggest event of its kind in the country. I grew up in a village just outside Lewes, and my mother never let me attend.

To a large extent, Phil's cause has indeed prevailed. The coalition government between the Liberal Democrats and the Conservatives that has emerged from the general election has just published its 11-point agreement, and under point number ten – "civil liberties" – are many of Phil's campaign issues. The coalition say they will scrap the ID card scheme, the national identity register, the next generation of biometric passports and the Contact Point database – a Jesuit-like state surveillance system aimed at tracking the development of every single child in Britain. The previous Labour government had overseen the proliferation of forensic DNA records and CCTV cameras until the UK had more of each than any other country in the world; the coalition government agreement included a pledge to regulate both these fields, as well as to check the amount of citizens' email and internet records being stored by the state.

It's no coincidence that the two parties who spent most of this time in opposition to New Labour came to government with a packet of database state reforms almost identical to Phil's wish-list. From the moment Gordon Brown came to power, sensible campaigners like Phil switched their lobbying efforts from the current government to the one they believed would succeed it. Phil recognises this success, "Our campaign certainly helped form the narrative of the coalition. The only common ground which the Conservatives and the Liberal Democrats probably didn't have to spend more than a couple of minutes around the table on in those four days in which they negotiated the agreement, was probably that section. It's roughly equivalent to the four or five demands that we've majored on, collectively." But he's under no illusions that his work is done, "Certainly I'm very happy. Very much happier than I have been for quite some time. I wouldn't say jubilant, because there's a lot of work to do simply to get what the politicians are saying actually enacted, and furthermore enforced."

The year New Labour came to power, 1997, was the same year that Larry Page and Sergey Brin registered the google.com domain name. One might therefore feel inclined to cut Labour a bit of slack if they didn't get new technology straight away. But the mistakes made over three terms of Labour government when it came to technology were awesome in scale. Many of them are comparatively well known: the unbelievable cost of major IT refits like the one botched by the Child Support Agency; the outrageous data security breach at HMRC that led to half the nation's bank details being leaked. But the cognitive metaphor that underlay many of these errors is less well known.

In 2002, fresh from a tour of a sheet-metal supplier in Huddersfield called Allsops, Tony Blair described to a conference of e-government experts his vision for the social justice supply-chain, a scaled-up version of Allsops' customer relations management system that would make public services more efficient. It would mark "a new relationship between citizen and state", with the added bonus that the massive contracts central government offered to build these new "citizen relationship management" systems, would re-stimulate a software industry in Britain destroyed by the millennial dotcom bust.

On deeper reflection, it should have been clear that a system for supplying customers with sheet metal might not scale to a system for delivering social justice. The "machine state" Tony Blair envisioned was a threat to privacy, that vital component of human dignity that keeps societies and communities going. "It is poor civic hygiene," wrote Bruce Schneier in his seminal 2000 work on computer security *Secrets and Lies*, "to install technologies that could someday facilitate a police state." Times change. Governments change. One day we might wake up, like Marcus and his friends in *Little Brother*, to find the technology we were told was put in place to serve us, suddenly turned against us.

Phil has been leading No2ID for six years, during which time he's worked both to seed a grassroots of hundreds of thousands of local campaigners and supporters and to lobby inside Whitehall and Westminster for a halt to the ID card scheme. I'm curious to know how he would describe what working that close to power feels like.

"I'm reminded of, I think it was *Manhunter*, the Michael Mann film, where the investigator is talking to Hannibal Lecter. Lecter is, as you know, an extremely intelligent sociopath. And he's talking to this guy called Will, and trying to understand how Will caught him. And it boiled down to Will saying 'but you had one major handicap: you are mad'. For me the Government were always onto a loser with ID cards because they were wrong and we were right - not in the sense of left/right politics. But simply because, I don't believe you can counter the assertion that I own me."

It's interesting – but perhaps not surprising given his prolonged exposure to the political system – that Phil's first reference point for government is a cannibalistic madman. But I'm guessing Phil's interpretation of what motivated his campaign's enemies is slightly more nuanced than this, and so I press further. Why, in his point of view, did they get it so wrong?

"I'm sure that none of them get up in the morning thinking 'Oh, I'll do bad things today'. In fact I'm sure it's exactly the opposite. I think they all get up, as I'm sure most people do in public life, thinking 'What can I do that's good and beneficial?' But there are serious problems in many of the things that they are doing. They are working from the basic assumption that 'we are the good people, therefore what we do for your benefit is for your benefit and can only be for your benefit, and we cannot see how that could be wrong'. That's a very dangerous attitude, especially with technology and especially given that so few politicians actually understand technology let alone how technology plays out in people's lives, at a societal level."

The people who really understand technology – the community at CCC, for example – might look anarchic, but they do at least understand and seek to help others understand just how important security and privacy are in the face of networked, digital technology. Indeed the German government often invite CCC to give expert testimony on technical issues. But in Britain, thanks in part Blair's ambition to use schemes like the National ID card to re-energise the tech industry after the dotcom bust, it was large technology consultancies like EDS and Capita – represented by the trade body Intellect – to whom the government went to for advice. And thanks to the millions of pounds at stake, such companies were always unlikely to be very critical of the government's plans.

But being self-critical is a crucial element of deploying good systems. "Here's a thought experiment I've suggested in the past," Phil continues. "When you are doing a privacy impact assessment for the design of a new system, if you cannot conceive and write down the way your system will kill someone then you haven't thought about privacy enough. Because virtually every massive centralised system imposed on a population is going to cause increasing amounts of problems for those people who don't fit the relatively narrow definition of 'the norm', or 'the way we want citizens to be'. I think many people will find themselves not just outliers, but actually positively disadvantaged by systems that make presumptions about the way they should live their lives. And some people will be harmed, possibly catastrophically. So if you start things on the premise that 'we are the good people and we're only doing it for your own good, and therefore the system that we're doing can only really be benign', that's just not enough."

What's worse, when vocal critics like Phil did come on the scene, instead of embracing and exploring such dissent, the civil servants at the Home Office closed them out completely. "The psychology that we have been opposing," Phil explains "has been a very entrenched one. It has been 'we are the good people, you are the anarcho-terrorists'. They quite literally wanted to think, certainly in the early stages, that No2ID, that this Phil Booth character, was just some sort of out-and-out nutter, some trouble maker. Certainly that was what they were talking about internally, as we discovered later. The Home Office was trying to prevent even other bits of government from talking to us and to me. That is really a very odd mentally. I mean, you are the Home Office. You are the establishment. You are the government. So why should a bunch of people who just got together because they disagreed with you on a policy or a programme that you were pursuing, why is it that they should pose so much of a threat?"

Being a campaigner can be very lonely. I know at ORG I was often the only person in the room from "civil society", that is, the only person not representing either the Government, or some commercial interest. Once, during a consultation on how best to protect children online, Yahoo!'s then full-time lobbyist – or 'Head of Public Policy' as they generally prefer to be known – actually queried why I was there at all. In what sense were the interests I represented different from the interests she was there to represent – that of her customers?

What this shows, and what I learned during my time at ORG, was that citizen involvement in day-to-day politics is a novelty in Westminster, and rather out of fashion. Politicians have become middle managers, administering an erratic and passive client base (the electorate) while reporting up to a corporately-funded multi-party system that long ago transformed from a scaffold for ideological discourse into a career development framework for awkward Oxbridge graduates. Citizenship has undergone what some scholars have called a process of "marketization". Benefits claimants and other users of public services are now "clients". MPs run their surgeries like pantomime social workers. Ministers appear on the *Today* programme to distribute their coupon-book soundbites for listeners to redeem on polling day. Re-imagined as consumers of a sanitised pre-watershed media concoction of "public life", citizens are no longer expected to behave in any other way than that which serves their own self-interest. The Digital Economy Bill got through at least partly because the MPs who received hundreds of letters from their constituents begging them not to pass it genuinely believed the only thing the authors of those letters cared about was their right to share music without paying for it.

This is one reason why government has come close to getting it wrong on internet regulation so often. Just like Bill Gates, government thinks that web users are not web-creators but web-consumers, and seeks to regulate the web as if it were a service being provided by companies like Google, Yahoo! and Facebook. More importantly, the fact that the digital age has come upon us halfway through our participatory shift from citizen to consumer also throws that shift into relief. Perhaps it would have been fine to stick with managerial-style politics had history really ended in 1989, but it didn't. Confronting completely new challenges to society – networked digital technology, climate change – perhaps we need a model that is a little more sophisticated than the Customer Helpdesk? Certainly, NO2ID's success at mobilising the grassroots indicates that citizen participation in public policy may not be the novelty Westminster believes it to be.

NO2ID don't actively seek to store a lot of information about the kind of people who support them. That would be more than a little hypocritical. "We don't count them!" laughs Phil, "But there are numbers you can float around. We're in the 90-100,000 supporters bracket if you like, and those are people to whom we send regular communication because they've asked us to. A relatively tiny proportion of those give us money on a regular basis. Over time, the support that we've had has been from people who are just very pissed off about it, getting out on a Saturday and handing out leaflets on a stall or something like that. Weekend after weekend after weekend – don't forget we've been going six years."

Nonetheless, over the years, through the work done by local groups' coordinators, they have noticed that a surprising number of people who are active in the NO2ID network, are otherwise uninterested in politics. "Because we weren't of one party or another, because we didn't come under a red or a yellow or a blue flag, it was just about the issue, that seemed to enable people to get involved politically who otherwise weren't."

Although it was championed by the Labour government, the database state is not a left/right issue. "It starts very simply with the principle that I own me," Phil explains. "At the heart of all these systems is the idea of the citizen as a suspect. It's not an abstract. It's being told you can't be trusted, it's being told what you can and can't do. It's being told you have to have an official identity. It's being told your kids are going to have to go on to this database. I guess if you looked at it from a completely neutral standpoint, opposition to that would tend to align you with small state values, it would tend to align you with liberal values, so that makes sense of why Conservatives and Liberal Democrats might have come on board. But it does also seem to chime with ideas about dignity and respect within the left. Of course, the left would tend to be seen as more statist: the welfare state, society, social engineering. But within that – you just need to look at the unions – its heart is about respect for the individual, respect for the working person, respect for the minorities. It's in there and I can't imagine there could be a coherent political party or a coherent political system that didn't have that somewhere because otherwise it would just be ultimately abhorrent to people. It just wouldn't work."

Just as political party membership has dwindled, there has been a dramatic rise among UK citizens of affiliation to single issue campaign networks. Since peak membership in the 1950s, political party membership across the UK's three major parties has declined by a factor of ten. Today, the National Trust has more members than the three parties put together. On the one hand, this could be interpreted as a consumer-like polity shopping for the issues about which they care most. But on the other, it is a clear indicator that the concerns of the political class no longer reflect those of society at large. What No2ID have achieved – in part at least, for there is still much work to be done – they have achieved in spite of the systems in place at Westminster and Whitehall to respond democratically to social challenges and social change. Campaign networks, and especially ones like No2ID, are more responsive, more inclusive and more representative than the MPs and bureaucrats we pay to keep society on the straight and narrow.

In 1984, Stewart Brand foresaw two challenges that the rise of networked digital technology would pose to societies. The first, that "information wants to be free", has undermined the copyright system set up in the printing press age, putting both innovation and free expression in jeopardy. The second, that "information wants to be expensive", that "the right information in the right place just changes your life" (and, conversely, the *wrong* information in the *wrong* place just changes your life too), continues to menace individuals' privacy, autonomy and dignity. On these issues, the instincts of the public have continuously outclassed the instincts of a political system compromised by its managerial self-image and its affinity with the corporate ethic. Westminster has, very publicly, come up wanting.

Phil began his working life as a public sculptor, later becoming a computer systems engineer to support his growing family. "I didn't really know much about the political system when I took on the No2ID National Coordinator role. I knew we had a Parliament and a House of Commons and MPs and a House of Lords and all that sort of stuff, but I didn't know how it worked. I don't think anyone can be proud of the system that we have here at present, but that doesn't mean that I have any real thought on what would be better. But everyone's admitting it – something is not right. I'm not going to say the system is completely and utterly broken. If it's so catastrophically broken we'd be in a far worse state than we are. But clearly, there are some systemic problems. There is something deeply wrong about the sort of entrenched attitudes and behaviours of the bureaucracy, at the heart of government, that seeks to serve its needs... And the waste! People talk about first-order waste – money that is being misspent. But the waste in this system is that so much of its effort is spent on perpetuating itself and attempting to do things that make it necessary. You know, the biggest surprise was how correct *Yes, Minister* was." Phil laughs, "It's all just vaguely disappointing."

We've left the pub and we're sunning ourselves and smoking roll-ups in the garden of Phil's modest ex-council home while his young son watches TV indoors. Phil continues, "What do I make of the political system? I just think, it is what it is." With his index and forefinger outstretched, he raises his hand and points to his temples. "I've got it in my head, you know? I've had to keep it in my head in order to be able to work out what we're doing. I'll be very glad, to be frank, to get it out of my head. I don't want to waste any more of my brain on having to understand it."

chapter

Chapter 6: Information Overload

It's now over a quarter of a century since Stewart Brand suggested that "information wants to be free", and around 15 years since John Perry Barlow released his *Declaration of the Independence of Cyberspace.* Are those of us who still take inspiration from these events simply living in the past? How does the development of the internet, the world wide web, the whole many-to-many communications kit and caboodle shape up against the expectations of the cyberspace pioneers and of those who followed them up onto the frontier?

Before that question can be answered, it's worth asking what those expectations were in the first place. 'Freedom' means lots of things to lots of people and, like any good PoMo kid, I only know for certain what it means to me. I grew up in an age where meaning – collective meaning, morals, ethics, religion etc – had fallen out of fashion. Without meaning, all that was left was the bottom line: everything beyond profit and loss was merely a matter of spin. Freedom to me meant space, yes, but it also meant finding a knowledge and a truth that could be more relied upon. Freeing information, taking it out of the hands of the intermediaries, be they governments, media conglomerates or corporate advertising executives, seemed like a good step on the way to that dream. I can't be sure, but I think that's also what John Perry Barlow meant by freedom when he talked about his "civilization of the Mind in Cyberspace... more humane and fair than the world your governments have made before."

When information can be reproduced at zero marginal cost, and spread around the world in an instant, it would seem sensible to hope that more knowledge will be put in the hands of more people, and that as a consequence, those who have benefitted from an education might be that bit wiser, and those who have not might be able to remedy their situation. As Jimmy Wales, the founder of Wikipedia, puts it, "Imagine a world in which every single person on the planet is given free access to the sum of all human knowledge. That's what we're doing."

When information is distributed not by an ever-shrinking group of global corporations guarding access to a one-way pipe, but by everyone, to everyone, so that it bursts like sunlight into every nook and cranny of the intellectual landscape, it would seem sensible to hope for a level of political and corporate transparency that might purge the world's elites of their most unsavoury elements. As US Supreme Court Justice and "People's

Lawyer" Louis Brandeis said in 1933, a phrase Barack Obama repeated in his first days as US President, "sunlight is the best disinfectant".

And when information communications technology enables motivated individuals to come together across geographic boundaries, to collaborate in building products like Linux and Wikipedia, products that each trump any equivalent the commercial world has to offer, then it would seem sensible to hope that the hegemony of the corporation, the growing dominance of an organisational model that has developed for the large part outside of our ideals of democracy and human rights, might be sent into remission. As Dr Emmett Brown once said to Marty McFly "Where we're going, we don't need roads".

It would seem sensible to hope all of these things. But have any of them actually happened?

On 21 January, around about the time I was sitting on Cory Doctorow's sofa talking back-to-the-land tech-Utopianism, Hilary Clinton, the US Secretary of State, delivered a lecture entitled *Remarks on Internet Freedom* at Washington DC's interactive Newseum complex.

Echoing Brand, Clinton started off her speech with the observation that "information has never been so free". She went on to name and shame certain regimes for their choice to censor the internet – China, Tunisia, Uzbekistan, Vietnam – and to praise the activities of the citizens of Iran, whose protests after the disputed re-election of President Mahmoud Ahmadinejad the previous year had gained a global audience via social networking sites like Twitter and Facebook.

Clinton announced significant US financial support for building censorship circumvention tools to help pro-democracy advocates in those countries access the materials being kept from them by their leaders. "On their own," she went on, "new technologies do not take sides in the struggle for freedom and progress. But the United States does." The speech alarmed many hackers who had already been working for years to create and distribute censorship circumvention tools. Had US foreign policy, with its attendant hypocrisies, hidden agendas and democratisation-by-force, now gone virtual?

The Open Net Initiative – a cross-continent collaboration between technology and security research institutions at the universities of Harvard, Cambridge, Oxford and Toronto – has been tracking internet censorship and state-level governance of cyberspace since 2001. In their 2008 report, *Access Denied*, they characterised the global state of internet filtering as concentrated in three regions, east Asia, the Middle East & north Africa, and central Asia, adding:

> Technical filtering does occur in other parts of the world, but in a more limited fashion, such as the internet filtering common in libraries and schools in the United States, child pornography filtering systems in northern Europe, and the filtering of Nazi paraphernalia and Holocaust denial sites in France and Germany.

By 2010, with the release of a new report, *Access Controlled*, the ONI's emphasis had changed. Now they argued that "internet censorship is becoming a global norm", with "many of the legal mechanisms that legitimate control over cyberspace... led by the advanced democratic countries of Europe and North America", and where "the industrialized North is establishing norms that are only too readily propagated and adopted by repressive and authoritarian regimes elsewhere".

EFF co-founder John Gilmore told *Time* magazine in 1993 that "The 'net interprets censorship as damage and routes around it." In the space between their two reports, the ONI had observed a shift in governments' approaches to controlling the information that circulates online. In 2008, when states were still using a broadcast model to understand the internet, with each website a channel that could be turned on and off, and each web user a viewer, Gilmore's observation held and state efforts to control the information environment didn't work. At the time, ONI observed that "the extent to which each person using the internet can at once be a consumer and a creator is particularly vexing to the broadcast-oriented censor". But as the state's model on the 'net became more sophisticated, so did its ability to control it. As the ONI put it in 2010:

> As the Internet has grown in political significance, an architecture of control — through technology, regulation, norms, and political calculus — has emerged to shape a new geopolitical information landscape.

The 2010 report describes how cyberspace, once thought to be outside the jurisdiction of John Perry Barlow's "weary giants of flesh and steel", is in fact being "colonized" by governments, and in particular by those governments like the US and China who have the most geopolitical and economic clout across the world. In the US and in other democracies, governments are using fear-invoking narratives of terrorism and child pornography as "convenient rubrics" for the wider goal of enforcing order in cyberspace through mass internet surveillance and filtering, even when cheaper and demonstrably more effective solutions were available. The ONI observe that:

> Across the OSCE, communities of practice in law enforcement, intelligence, and the private sector are working, often in uncoordinated, discrete, but like-minded ways, leading to a normalization of Internet surveillance and censorship across all sectors of cyberspace. It is perhaps ironic that these norms so antithetical to basic rights and freedoms are being propagated from many countries that just over a decade ago were responsible for the expansion of liberal democratic principles and market capitalism across the globe.

Indeed the irony is that although Hilary Clinton might preach, as she did in her Newseum speech in January, that "Today, we find an urgent need to protect these freedoms on the digital frontiers of the 21st century," what she practises can appear to be quite different.

Much of the software used to aid censorship regimes in the Middle East, or the hardware originally commissioned to build China's Great Firewall, is made in the good old US of A. Google may be publicly wringing its hands over whether to supply censored search services to mainland China, but there are plenty of other companies in Silicon Valley quite happy to do business with repressive regimes, including Secure Computing, (whose parent company, McAfee, was bought by Intel in 2010 for around £5bn), who provide custom lists of socially and politically sensitive web URLs to Middle Eastern and north African autocrats, and Cisco, who build routers with baked-in censorship and surveillance capacity for state ISPs in China. But companies often end up developing these products not because they spot a gap in the market to prop up dictatorships, but because US state and federal governments have requested this functionality themselves, to prevent pupils from accessing "inappropriate" content on their school networks, or to provide national security agencies with their own surveillance backdoors. More recently, through the law courts and also through national and supra-national legislative efforts, internet service providers in the West are being asked to develop and install such censorship and surveillance equipment to identify and block peer-to-peer filesharers. In our IP-obsessed world, copyright-infringing teenagers are the logical next entry after terrorists and paedophiles on the list of society's most hated.

The ONI are worried about all this surveillance activity, which they see as "much more extensive and penetrating" than the "globe-spanning electronic surveillance systems" operated by the United States and the Soviet Union throughout the Cold War. They characterise state surveillance, alongside counter-information and targeted cyber attacks on political opponents as part of a new generation of internet controls that enhance state control over national cyberspace. "Cyberspace has become militarized", they write, "the prospect of an arms race in cyberspace looms large."

Senator Clinton's speech lasted just under an hour, but it reverberated around the news media for many months after it was delivered. At the end, Imam Mohamed Magid, a Muslim community organiser from Virginia, stood up and asked Mrs Clinton whether young people who disagreed with US foreign policy could also find space to express themselves online. Here's Clinton's response:

> I agree with you completely, sir, that not only young people in the Muslim world, but young people across the world are increasingly disconnected from authority, from government, from all kinds of institutions that have been historically the foundations of society, because they are so interconnected through the internet... There are so many manipulators online right now, not just stoking the anxieties and the fears of Muslim youth, but youth everywhere... So we have our own work to do, not just through our government but through our families, through our education systems, and every other institution to make sure we understand the power of this technology and to engage with young people through it and about it.

Whatever it was Senator Clinton had in mind when she made her internet freedom speech, it probably wasn't WikiLeaks.

It's only in early June that I understand what I missed when I turned down Rop's offer to go to Iceland. The *New Yorker* prints a long-form feature by Raffi Khatchadourian, a writer who embedded with the WikiLeaks team in the weeks running up to the *Collateral Murder* video release. In it, he describes the house Rop and Julian rented in Reykjavik near the North Atlantic coast under the guise of journalists pretending to cover the volcanic ash cloud story:

> After the owner left, Assange quickly closed the drapes, and he made sure that they stayed closed, day and night. The house, as far as he was concerned, would now serve as a war room; people called it the Bunker.

Reading the *New Yorker* piece, my suspicions were confirmed: WikiLeaks were indeed the radicals I was looking for back in Berlin. Khatchadourian describes them as a "media insurgency", an underground network of individuals – some only known to each other by code names. They traffic in information, samizdat that threatens not only dictators in countries far away, but corrupt businessmen, politicians and public servants in liberal democracies closer to home. They risk their own personal safety, driven by a higher cause.

But will we ever preserve Julian, Rop and their co-conspirators in Reykjavik behind glass, celebrate them as we do the hip young agitators of communist East Germany? If Julian was right when he told me that, at least in the West, speech is free because it really doesn't make that much of a difference to the way power works, then what, exactly, can WikiLeaks hope to achieve? History is written by the winners, and the emotive retelling of the fall of Communism ultimately serves a political purpose. Perhaps WikiLeaks fit better into the Baader-Meinhof shaped compartment of our cultural memory? But they're not terrorists. They're not killing anyone. They're simply getting out the truth. WikiLeaks confuse us because they look like a revolution, albeit one predicated on information, not violence. And you shouldn't need a revolution in a democracy.

Collateral Murder is made up of classified footage, recorded in 2007 from the cockpit of a US Army helicopter as it fired on and killed two unarmed Reuters journalists in an eastern district of Baghdad. Through the gunsights we see the men, along with half a dozen or so others, run for their lives from the US heavy weaponry. The voiceover, provided by the men inside the helicopter and their radio contacts, sounds like young men playing a computer game together. As the fight progresses, eleven of those on the ground die. Two children waiting in a van close by are seriously wounded.

The day *Collateral Murder* launched, it created a media storm, with coverage in every major international newspaper, and a long segment on MSNBC. Robert Gates, the US Defense Secretary, was forced to respond and his response fell flat (the video showed a view of the war "through a soda straw", with "no before and no after"). But over the following days, as news outlets developed the story using their official connections to bring in talking heads with military expertise, the message behind the video slowly evaporated. WikiLeaks were accused – probably fairly – of editorialising the footage, and failing to draw attention to surrounding gunfights and a rocket-propelled grenade launcher (RPG) being held by one of the group talking to the journalists. Commentators also focussed on whether it was possible to mistake a long-lens camera, like the one the ill-fated journalists were carrying, for another RPG. WikiLeaks put out a 140-character response on Twitter:

> STOP SPINNING. Permission to kill everyone in Iraq vid was asked for, and granted, BEFORE any mention of "RPG".

But to no avail.

A lot of people like to blame the destruction of the media on the internet. 2010 was also the year Rupert Murdoch put the online version of *The Times* newspaper behind a paywall, having decreed that his customers were "smart enough to know they can't get something for nothing". But in truth, the quality of news journalism was falling fast way before the rise of the web. As Nick Davies recounts in his excellent polemic against the modern news machine *Flat Earth News*, old-school newspaper proprietors of the sixties and seventies were focussed at least to some extent on quality investigative journalism. But they soon gave way to businessmen owners in the eighties and nineties who cared more for the bottom line. Both breeds of newspaper magnate used their printed organs to promote their own political interests. But only the latter made journalism "competitive", squeezing operations until they could undercut and destroy their rivals. This both consolidated their influence on the public sphere, and relegated most print news output to "churnalism" – rehashed press releases and wire copy. Journalists began relying too heavily on their relationships with insider contacts for fresh political stories, had no time or resource to delve into a story, or to uncover the nuances of a debate beyond the usual talking points. Three days after the release of *Collateral Murder*, WikiLeaks tweeted the following:

> Raised >$150K in donations since Mon. New funding model for journalism: try doing it for a change.

Collateral Murder begins with a quote from George Orwell, "Political language is designed to make lies sound truthful and murder respectable, and to give the appearance of solidity to pure wind." Although it wasn't meant to, this phrase also serves as an epitaph for the video WikiLeaks worked so hard to put out in the public domain. Still, although the message behind the video only needed a light breeze to be carried out of the media echo chamber and disappear into the ether, WikiLeaks themselves remained in the headlines throughout the spring and into summer. In early June, *Wired* magazine's *Threat Level* blog was the first to report the arrest of a junior US Army analyst in Baghdad. Private Bradley Manning, 22, was being held in Kuwait under suspicion of leaking the video and other classified documents to WikiLeaks.

WikiLeaks had been on the US government's radar long before the *Collateral Murder* video. In 2008, the US Army Counterintelligence Center produced an internal memo entitled *Wikileaks.org—An Online Reference to Foreign Intelligence Services, Insurgents, or Terrorist Groups?*, essentially a briefing for US intelligence officials on the site. As well as detailing its activities and potential ambitions, the memo posited ways to undermine WikiLeaks. Chief among these was the suggestion that:

> Successful identification, prosecution, termination of employment and exposure of persons leaking the information by the governments and businesses affected by information posted to Wikileaks.org would damage and potentially destroy this center of gravity and deter others from taking similar actions.

The counterintelligence document had been leaked to and published by WikiLeaks in March 2010. As the Bradley Manning story hit the headlines, several commentators observed that prosecution of the young Private would appear to present the US government with exactly the opportunity they had been seeking. Manning is now awaiting trial in the US. If found guilty of leaking classified documents, he could face up to 52 years in prison.

The story of how Manning came to the attention of the US authorities is shot through with the names of famous computer hackers. Kevin Poulsen, the *Wired* reporter responsible for *Threat Level*, is a convicted hacker who reinvented himself as a journalist in the late nineties after his release from a four-year prison term for computer fraud. Poulsen's source Adrian Lamo, the man who turned Manning over to the authorities after he was alleged to have confessed his whistle-blowing activity on an instant message chat, had pleaded guilty to charges of computer crime in 2004, leading to a suspended sentence and two years' probation. Why Manning revealed himself to Lamo is unknown. Lamo has admitted that he offered Manning journalist-source confidentiality before the young soldier confessed, an offer upon which Lamo evidently reneged.

Both Lamo and Poulsen appear on lists of the top ten most famous hackers of all time. Clearly both still like making "interesting trouble". Rumours that Lamo is now working on asymmetrical information warfare tactics on behalf of the United States National Security Agency remain unconfirmed. Most probably they always will.

After *Collateral Murder*, Julian Assange went into hiding. But just over a month after Bradley Manning's story hit the headlines, at noon on 25 July, he appeared again, fronting a press conference at London's Frontline Club for WikiLeaks' second high-profile leak of the year: the Afghan War Logs, around 75,000 classified internal US field reports sent from the war in Afghanistan.

This time, Julian was only appearing to answer questions. There was no video to show, no secrets to dramatically reveal, because the story was already out there. That morning, Germany's *Der Spiegel,* the UK *Guardian* and *The New York Times* had simultaneously published multiple-page exposés on the scandals the new leaked material revealed: that an unacceptably high rate of civilian casualties was being deliberately hidden by NATO forces; that it was well-known that Pakistan, ostensibly an ally to NATO, was secretly funding the enemy Taliban with US money; that the Taliban were armed with much more sophisticated weaponry than was ever made public.

Back when I'd spoken to him in Berlin, Daniel Schmitt had talked about the difficulties WikiLeaks had had in engaging with mainstream newspapers. Though the information they found themselves in possession of was very often highly scandalous, it was also incredibly dense. And because no newspaper had exclusive access to it, that is, because WikiLeaks made it publicly available online, the "scoop" incentive for any commercial newspaper to invest time in trawling the material for stories was perceived as absent. The economics of newspaper production meant much of the most salacious material went unreported.

The Afghan War Logs project turned that trend around. So it was a little surprising that Julian chose to take centre stage on the day of the Afghan War Logs publication by holding an hour-long press conference at the Frontline Club. When I'd prodded him for information on his personal background during our interview at Chaos, he sounded like the kind of guy who didn't want to take centre stage, who would prefer to let the material speak for itself. What had happened to change his mind?

Very quickly, the story of the Afghan War Logs became the story of Julian Assange. The same American TV channels brought out the same military talking heads, most of whom told the news anchors that the material released by WikiLeaks was "nothing new". And of course to anyone, like them, with security clearance – the *Washington Post* recently reported that a whopping 854,000 people hold top secret clearance in the US – it was nothing new. But to the people who didn't have such clearance, very often the ones sending their sons and daughters to war in Afghanistan, the picture painted by the Afghan War Logs may well not have matched their ideas about the conflict.

Just a day or so after the release of the Afghan War Logs, the US State Department accused WikiLeaks of publishing the names of key Afghan informants in a few of the 75,000 reports on their website, exposing them to reprisals from the Taliban. The Australian *Times* claimed on 28 July that:

> In just two hours of searching the Wikileaks archive, *The Times* found the names of dozens of Afghans credited

> with providing detailed intelligence to US forces. Their villages are given for identification and also, in many cases, their fathers' names.

Although there have been no reports of revenge attacks, on 29 July, three days after the biggest leak in military history uncovered hundreds of previously unreported civilian casualties at the hands of NATO forces, the chairman of the US Joint Chiefs of Staff Admiral Mike Mullen was still able to accuse Julian Assange of having "blood on his hands". The story was lapped up by the international press. An editorial in the *Washington Post* labelled WikiLeaks a criminal, if not a terrorist, enterprise and called for the Obama administration to circumvent international law and "employ not only law enforcement but also intelligence and military assets to bring Assange to justice and put his criminal syndicate out of business."

Like thousands if not millions of people across the world, I was engrossed by these twists and turns in events. The character of Julian Assange as it was gradually painted – by the international press, by political officials, the commentariat, the bloggers and tweeters, the people I met in pubs who discussed WikiLeaks in wide-eyed terms – merged bit-by-bit with the man I met in Berlin until I could no longer be sure which picture was real. Beyond the odd off-record connection – a snatched conversation with an old journalist contact who had recently dined with friends in London who were harbouring Julian, a report from an activist friend of a chance meeting at Frontline – I drank mainly from the firehose of reaction to

WikiLeaks' activities that gushed into the public sphere, until I was inebriated.

I became just another voyeur. In the comfort of my study in a pretty English village, I poured myself a coffee, logged on, and tuned out, happy simply to blow my mind with the acceleration and scale of events.

What I find most shocking about all this is how two stories – the *Collateral Murder* video, and the Afghan War Logs – which each had the power to rock the US military-industrial complex to its very foundations, were instead defused with such relative ease. And I, as one member of the international audience, am complicit in that scandal. There's a reason this book isn't about the shocking abuse of military power by the US and UK against states and citizens in the Middle East, about the "fiscalisation" of power, the privatisation of authority and the whole geopolitical chess game. Apparently, I'd rather spend my time thinking about freedom in the abstract, talking to nice, safe hippies about the dreams some of them had once and what happened to them. I don't regret my decision to write myself out of this story, to decline the invitation to Reykjavik. It turns out I'm not any kind of revolutionary.

The hopes that many held for the redemptive potential of the internet lay in the fact that the internet was a disintermediating force. The many-to-many communications environment would allow individuals to bypass outmoded cultural gatekeepers and to smash corrupt institutions. The assumption was twofold – that those institutions would be unable to fight back, and that the ordinary people at the bottom of society, the edges of the network, were somehow worthier than the centralised elites at the top. Internet thinkers like to talk about "network effects", about how networks that connect everyone to everyone double in value each time they add one more connection, how the value of a network, and thus its power, can increase exponentially and at a rapid pace. WikiLeaks takes advantage of this feature, and attempts to exploit it in pursuit of truth. But it works both ways. The crowd isn't always wise. Courage isn't always contagious. The WikiLeaks story also shows how easy it remains to distract the masses.

chapter 7

learning to love the Google

Chapter 7: Learning to love the Goolag

It's early July, and I'm in the bar of London's Frontline Club, waiting for Ethan Zuckerman. From where I'm sitting in the room of sun-soaked wood panelling, I can see a glass case containing pictures of war correspondents. But although it looks like a school notice board, really it's a shrine: every smiling face now behind that glass was killed in action sometime in the last twenty years. The Frontline Club was co-founded by video journalist Vaughan Smith, and Smith is one of only two founding members of Frontline Television News not in that glass case. Established amid the chaos of the Romanian revolution in 1989, Frontline Television News was a collective of journalists pushing the technological and operational limits of war reporting. In 2003, Vaughan Smith converted the organisation into the members club it is today. The food served in the restaurant downstairs is sourced almost exclusively from the remote Norfolk farm where Smith now lives.

Frontline's stylish, leather-and-wood interior is a reminder of how conflict can lurk beneath the surface of things that otherwise seem quite normal and everyday. I've been a member of the Frontline Club for just over a year, and a visitor for many more years than that. And yet it is only as my visits have accumulated that I've come to notice and understand the ephemera that coat the walls and staircases of this four-storey building around the corner from Paddington station. Those boots in that glass case are boots that once belonged to William Howard Russel, correspondent to *The Times* during the Crimean War. The reception desk is in fact a display cabinet, housing Vaughan Smith's mobile phone shot through with bullets on a mission in Serbia. A Moroccan-style rug that decorates one of the attic bedrooms looks innocuous in its colonial pastiche until you notice its motif is tanks, guns and grenades. At the Frontline Club, war is not a remote and alien thing, a dreamscape played out on the *Nine O'Clock News*.

As you would expect, the club has several excellent photography displays. From St Paul's Cathedral rising up from the fog of the Blitz to photos of where the Twin Towers once stood on September 11, the permanent collection includes work by Robert Capa, Larry Burrows, Marc Riboud and Jeff Wedener. It was originally curated by John G Morris, a man who worked as picture editor for *Life* magazine during World War II, and who went on to work as the founding picture editor for Magnum Photos. In the introduction to the collection on the Frontline website, he writes:

> We decided to pull no punches. We wanted to compel you, the members and guests of Frontline, to think of the risk taken by those who took the pictures and also to think about those who were photographed. Sorry if such thoughts spoil your lunch.

In less than a fortnight, Julian Assange will be in this building, waiting to speak to the press about the Afghan War Logs.

The man I'm waiting for today, Massachusetts-based hacker and scholar Ethan Zuckerman, is also a man who wants to take people outside their comfort zones and make them think. In 2004, along with journalist and China expert Rebecca MacKinnon, Ethan founded Global Voices, an international network of multilingual citizen journalists that works to get reporting from non-Western parts of the world more exposure on the web. While he was still a student at Williams College in Williamstown, Massachusetts, Ethan had co-founded the online community-hosting portal Tripod.com, which sold to Lycos in the late nineties. On graduation, Ethan spent a year in Ghana on a Fulbright scholarship before returning to the United States at the turn of the Millennium to found GeekCorps, a kind of VSO for geeks which sends people with technical skills to the developing world to help with computer-related projects.

Ethan now works out of the Berkman Center for Internet and Society, a mecca for internet intellectuals at Harvard Law School, and one of the four partner institutions that make up the Open Net Initiative. Ethan has regularly been engaged in major research on online censorship and censorship circumvention, often of a very technical nature. And he's maintained a love of and expertise in African media and technology development – his blog is called "My heart's in Accra". Today, Ethan is on his way from Massachusetts to Nigeria via the TED Global conference that has just wound up in Oxford. He's agreed to meet me here for an hour or two before he catches the Heathrow express train from Paddington station, just across the road.

Eventually, Ethan appears in the narrow doorframe at the bar's entrance, his huge form augmented by some serious luggage. He's been waiting outside, unsure of the etiquette of this private members club. As usual, he's jovial and undaunted, his Massachusetts manners putting even this Englishwoman to shame. We settle down to drinks.

"The reason I think internet freedom is interesting and potentially useful," Ethan explains, "Is not because I believe some sort of Marxist-Leninist revolution is round the corner based on IT. If anything, I think a sort of an Anglo-American revolution might be long around the corner."

For a moment, I have no idea what he is talking about. Ethan smiles at me. "I mean when we broke free of your shackles, through the long arduous public debate process of trying to figure out what a better government would be than the lousy one we had." I realise he's talking about the 18th century. I feel slightly embarrassed, but Ethan lets it go with a wave of his hand.

Ethan is worried that the virtual places we're creating online to foster such a debate are not what they seem. "That forces us to think about how we create public spaces. [With the web] we think we have a free and open space to communicate in. Well maybe we don't. Because it *is* owned and controlled, and because of that it's possible that certain types of speech actually get very difficult."

When the WELL went online, the internet was very much a network of ends, and for that reason people believed that the 'net, and later the web, had a radical potential to refresh public discourse. No longer would debate be led by media oligopolies brokering access to a one-way pipe. The consolidation of media, epitomized by Rupert Murdoch's News International empire, could not happen over this network. Or so went the theory.

In fact today, according to a company called Arbor Networks who have access to a significant majority of the world's internet traffic, about 60% of all web traffic terminates at about 150 companies, and about 30% of all web traffic terminates at about 30 companies. 6% of web traffic is the result of just one company: Google. Consolidation in cyberspace has already happened, and in a remarkably shorter timeframe than the consolidation of print and broadcast media. Just like our local high street, a once-thriving marketplace of independent ventures is being taken over by familiar and deodorised corporate giants – Facebook, Yahoo!, Amazon, YouTube. How has this happened?

"The rhetoric of the internet early on was this massively decentralised network where every point routes to every point," Ethan explains. "It doesn't matter if you cut the wires it will reroute around it and everything is sort of an independent end node, right? Technically things are fairly independent as end nodes. You can do ludicrous things with just a PC attached to this network. And the whole rise of peer-to-peer [filesharing] demonstrates how ludicrous you can be just doing peers.

"The first thing to note is that it's nowhere near as resilient as we promised ourselves it was. You know, when a cable goes down in west Africa it has very real, very significant consequences. But what turns out to be most interesting, at least for me, is that we thought all the services would be at the edge of the networks. Which is to say lots of people would have their own web servers under their control, their own mail servers under their control. And what's been happening gradually over about 15 years is everyone has said, 'that's really a pain in the ass and I really don't want to do that.'"

Much like the sixties communards who gave up farming the land after one season showed them how hard it was, communicatory self-sufficiency turned out to be a bit of a drag. "I think it changed first because of spam," Ethan says. "Basically, if you run your own mail server these days the amount of time you have to spend training your spam filter is just insane. And so I would say 80% of the sort of hardcore geeks I know just moved over to Gmail, and have just sort of said, 'It's fine. You know? Yes, now Google controls my email. If I really am worried about it I can always encrypt on top of it, but the pain I'm going through to maintain my own mail server just isn't worth it anymore'." Ethan and I both use Gmail.

"After that," Ethan continues, "we started to see consolidation of web hosting. And similarly that's more of a cost issue. Web traffic is really spikey. And what you really want to do is to be able to turn up the bandwidth to your server. Or potentially put another server in if you're having a good day and suddenly everyone's paying attention to you. That's really hard to do if you're off on your own running your own box. So a lot of people have moved to using hosted web services. Those web services tend to converge and so you end up with companies like Rackspace which now control large percentages of the independent web.

"Where this has really gotten crazy is in social media. Social media is almost by definition heavily centralised." Ethan says the reason for this is "it's a namespace problem", which is a short and rather technical way of saying that we need directories like Facebook and Twitter to make it easy for us to find our friends online among the sea of people who share their names. Just as the Screen Actors Guild and Equity stipulate that no two of their members may have the same stage name to avoid confusion, Facebook and Twitter make sure no two of their users have the same handle or identifying code, meaning you can always find the exact Ethan Zuckerman or Becky Hogge you're looking for.

What all this means is that although the rhetoric behind the 'net was one of radical decentralisation, disintermediation and the chance at a truly plural public sphere, the reality of it pens us into what are essentially a handful of corporate pseudo-public spaces.

"It's terrifying," says Ethan. "And the reason it's terrifying is that much of the thinking that we've done about the internet is thinking about open standards, autonomous agents, all able to make our own decisions. But if you are using a social media platform or a blogging platform to publish your thoughts, you are within one of these large spaces. At a certain point, you are dependent on their rules of the road for your continued existence."

Ethan found himself thinking about this problem for the first time when friends of his in Zimbabwe, a human rights organisation called Kubatana, were told by their hosting provider Bluehost, one of the largest hosting providers in the US, that they had to go. When Kubatana asked Bluehost why, the response was simple but shocking: "because you're Zimbabwean."

What had happened was this. The US Department of Trade maintains a list of sanctioned individuals in Zimbabwe with whom US companies are prevented from doing business, and the penalties for violating those sanctions had been slowly ratcheting up over the last few years. At some point Bluehost's lawyers had apparently decided that, legal niceties aside, it probably wasn't worth their while serving any Zimbabweans. The edict had gone out "Get rid of the Zimbabweans. They're not worth it."

"So what happened," Ethan recounts, "was well after Kubatana had signed up to their account, Bluehost changed their terms of service." Most 'net companies reserve the right to change their terms of service at any time, often without notifying the users who unwittingly agree to abide by them. "Their new terms of service state, 'I am not a Zimbabwean' or Syrian or Cuban or any number of other countries. And so my friends were being kicked out for being Zimbabwean. Now, if you're a human rights activist in Zimbabwe, this is a pretty easy fight as far as they go. So they decided to start a fight. They got the US Embassy in Harare to call the Treasury Department and have the Treasury Department call this company and say, 'You idiots, fix this'. And so three weeks later after much nasty email exchanges there was an apology from the CEO inviting them back." At which point, according to Ethan, they said what they had intended to say all along, namely, "Go fuck yourself." They now host with Verio.

The Open Net Initiative published a report in 2010 detailing the practices of five major social networking and blogging platforms – Facebook, YouTube, Flickr, Twitter and Blogger – and the effects these practices were having on free speech. Based on these investigations, the report speculated that Facebook was using a crude, numbers-based system for policing its content, automatically deactivating accounts and group pages if a threshold of complaints was met. It also identified specific Facebook groups who were gaming this system, for example a group of Arab Muslims whose stated aim was to get the account of every atheist Arab deleted by Facebook's automated system. Although YouTube was found to offer better avenues of redress to users who felt their content had been removed unfairly, ONI discovered anecdotal evidence to show that it too set the threshold of permitted speech far higher than one might expect of, say, serious broadcasting. YouTube had deleted a number of human rights videos – mostly from the Arab world – on the basis of the violence and illegal activity they depicted, rather than the context in which those depictions were being communicated. Flickr too, had come up against human rights activists

– this time in Romania – angry at content removed from their streams.

The ONI are not anti-capitalists. They make clear in the introduction to their report that they understand that corporations who provide services like YouTube and Facebook are working under competing pressures: the pressure to create a viable business, to keep their services available in countries with restrictive laws, and the pressure to avoid politically-motivated cyber-attacks on their infrastructure from groups keen to suppress ideas through force. "Negotiating this terrain often means compromising," they write, "sometimes at the expense of users".

Nonetheless, the ONI also rightly identify the current state of affairs as deeply precarious. Because the platforms they investigated are beginning to dominate online communications, the efforts these platform operators make to police their own content will have a substantial and growing impact on free expression and public discourse:

> As users flock toward popular social media sites such as Facebook and Twitter, they are effectively stepping away from public streets and parks and into the spaces analogous and similar in some respects to shopping malls – spaces that are privately owned and often subject to stringent rules and lacking in freedoms.

As Ethan puts it, "it's sort of like saying, 'let's go have a good public argument about this. And we'll do it at Terminal 5 at Heathrow'. If what's interesting about internet freedom is this idea of creating digital public spaces where we can debate whatever issues are relevant. And if what's exciting about internet freedom is that countries that don't have conventional public spaces could now have digital public spaces, then we have to recognise, those aren't public spaces. Those are private spaces; those are corporate-controlled spaces."

In *No Logo*, Naomi Klein details exactly what's wrong with the real-world emergence of pseudo-public space in corporate America:

> The conflation of shopping and entertainment found at the superstores and theme-park malls has created a vast grey area of pseudo-public private space. Politicians, police, social workers and even religious leaders all recognize that malls have become the modern town square. But unlike the old town squares, which were and still are sites for community discussion, protests and political rallies, the only type of speech that is welcome here is marketing and other consumer patter. Peaceful protestors are routinely thrown out by mall security guards for interfering with shopping, and even picket lines are illegal inside these enclosures.

It's ironic that a technology that gave citizens the ability to take back public space and public discourse from corporate control could have turned so quickly into the anti-globalisation movement's worst nightmare – a virtual corporate beast a hundred times more efficient than anything in the real world at exploiting the citizen-consumer's own expression and desire in order to sell advertising. Why did things pan out so differently to the way early geeks expected them to?

"This was such an anti-corporate space when a lot of people were starting to play with it for the first time," says Ethan. "If your first internet experience was the WELL, you might have asked, 'Who the hell's going to make money off a bunch of Grateful Dead fans?' My first experience was Usenet. And the notion that someone was somehow going to make money off that cesspool seemed utterly ludicrous. Back then, I'd always assumed that when we were promising investors that we'd do good things with their money that, you know, we were probably going to lose money hand over fist. So it's never made any sense to me."

Ethan is thinking back to his Tripod.com days, before the big sale to Lycos. "In the nineties, we were these scrappy little youngsters in a house in Williamstown, Massachusetts, with no affiliations to big companies. And the companies that were big, and that we admired, had silly names like Yahoo! and their founders rode around on skateboards. So it was hard to think of this as the big corporate consolidation. It looked like the internet was this space where anyone could do anything with very few resources and a very low start-up cost. And in fact that does seem to continue to sort of be true. You know, Twitter was able to become Twitter pretty damn fast. So I think maybe it is still a pretty open space. In that, if you can create a platform and convince people that they want to be on it you are free to do that. But I think it is a space that naturally consolidates. And I think it consolidates because of brand."

So much for *No Logo*. Ethan explains, "When geography no longer matters, brand matters a lot more. I remember people saying in 1998, 'I want to be the number one retailer in the online pet and pet food space.' It turns out that there is no online pet and pet foods space. There's an online retail space, Amazon is number one at it. Being number two at it isn't very helpful. But I think that was hard to call. And I think it was hard to call, because the myth of the garage entrepreneur doesn't seem like it is about centralisation."

Though we started with water, Ethan and I have moved on to beer, and I'm feeling a little bold. What, I ask him, does this tell us about us? After all, evil forces are not at play here. The internet actually resisted regulatory interference from the old order in quite an amazing way, at least in its early years. Were we always unlikely to match up to the net's potential?

Ethan takes a sip of his drink and thinks. "We're sitting near the heart of a city of, how many million people?"

I tell him ten, although I'm none too sure.

"That's a lot of people..." he says.

"That *is* a lot of people," I reply.

"And they've decided to get together in a fairly close environment. The real estate here, the permission to use this piece of land we're sitting on, it's a whole lot more expensive than in some other parts of this country. Human beings like being together. And we have this natural tendency to get together. In fact we're watching this happen across the world right now. We're urbanising and we're urbanising very quickly because when people get together there's more opportunity, there's more excitement. You know there's just *more*, the closer you get together. I think centralisation is in the human spirit. And

I think what's interesting is this. You know the reason why London doesn't have one giant Sainsbury's? It's geography. We couldn't all get to it. And if we could, we couldn't all get *through* it, right? You know, we'd all end up fighting over the iceberg lettuce and you'd never get to the rocket. And there'd be a big, big problem. The internet lets us all go to Sainsbury's at the same time, and we can all get our lettuce at the same time. And at a certain point the question then becomes, well why not just have one Sainsbury's?"

Like Frontline's founder, Vaughan Smith, neither Ethan nor I live in a city. He lives in rural Massachusetts with his wife and son, a three-hour drive out of Boston. I live in an area of Cambridgeshire that produces a significant proportion of the vegetables Sainsbury's stocks on its shelves. But we're the exception, not the rule. In global terms, we're ludicrously wealthy – in the top 1%. We're running off to rural areas because we believe that when we get there, we'll be free. Perhaps for the same reason, we both fell prey to the excitement of decentralisation promised by the 'net.

"We're Utopians," Ethan says.

Ethan's wife is studying to become a Rabbi. Prophecy is a regular topic of conversation in their household. Ethan tells me that Old Testament prophets were very bad about predicting the future. "They all predicted that fire would rain from the sky and that unless people did this and this we'd never have the shining city of God." But thinking that prophets predict the future is, Ethan says, a really shallow and immature way to do prophecy. The way to read prophets is as a challenge, as a challenge to you to make the changes to get to wherever it is you want to be, be that the Shining City of God or the Civilisation of Mind.

"So if you read it as prophecy and not as prediction, if you read into him as a prophet, in that sense of a prophet," Ethan goes on, "John Perry Barlow isn't completely crazy. He's saying, 'here is what we could have, now let's do the work to get there.' And he's not being all that unreasonable. I actually think it's great to go back and look at these texts and ask, are these values still my values? A lot of these values are still my values. So then you ask yourself, 'OK, what if I wanted to live these values? What would need to change?' That's what I'm working on now."

Ethan's been very kind in focussing in on my preoccupations during this interview, but he's actually most concerned with a different problem at the moment. The talk he's just given at the TED Global conference in Oxford has made significant headlines. The challenge he set up Global Voices to face – to spread the ideas of a wider proportion of the world's population than the Western mainstream media currently reflect – is becoming bigger than ever. Far from connecting us to people in the world with whom we would otherwise have no immediate connection, the web is ploughing us deeper into our own cultural furrows.

According to Ethan, right now, web users are suffering from a kind of imaginary cosmopolitanism. Although the network reaches the farthest corners of the world, culturally we the users of the network tend to inhabit the bits of it with which we're already familiar. Geographically, the attention that for example, audiences in the United States invest in different parts of the world, looks the same across television news, high-end newspaper news *and* new forms of web-based expression like Wikipedia. It's all rich countries (the US, Europe, Japan) and "countries we've invaded," Ethan says. The connections made on Facebook between, say, Israelis and Palestinians, are dwarfed by the connections made within these groups, or with Israelis and Americans or Palestinians and other Arabs. If we don't make a concerted effort to "widen our web", and soon, then the network may only serve to reinforce our cultural biases. The rest of the world may only be a click away, but if we don't act positively to make that click, they will be as removed as ever.

"Most of the early internet values are good values – the idea that we are independent actors with rights in this space, that we are political participants in this space. The idea that we do want this space to be a more level playing field than the real world, that we want it to be cosmopolitan. Those are all really good ambitions. It just turns out that they don't happen automatically."

This is the bad news for internet Utopianism. Stewart Brand and his band of merry hippies, the hackers who convened in the early eighties in Germany and America, Cory Doctorow and his next generation of hip, code-toting activists, Julian Assange and the purveyors of radical free speech at WikiLeaks: if something links all these groups it is the fire which the promise of a decentralized, liberated communications system ignited in their bellies. Their belief, that there was something inherent in such a new technology, something "automatic" that could sweep aside stagnant and underperforming institutions, failed to take into account the fact that the society that created those institutions had its own irresistible forces. Seductive as the image of the lone hacker taking down the system is, the web is, ultimately a reflection of its users. Online, the vanguard has long ago been joined by the rest of the world, and the rest of the world didn't get John Perry Barlow's memo.

It costs about $6,000 to attend a major TED conference like TED Global as a delegate. Although the contract he signed as a speaker means Ethan is not at liberty to disclose publicly who he's met this year at Oxford, he tells me that at previous TEDs he has seen "incredibly famous people", mentioning both a former US Presidential candidate and an A-List Hollywood actor. Venture capitalists also turn out in force, and as well as thinkers like Ethan (he says he "had a good TED"), the speakers they turn up to hear include ambitious young start-up companies. Speaking at TED is a business plan. "Your audience includes a lot of CEOs and a lot of investors. The pressure is incredibly high."

Because of the high ticket price, TED is often perceived as elitist, so much so that a rival free conference, "BIL", now shadows the official TED conference, offering unscheduled talks that anyone can give by day, and the chance to "hang around the area the TEDsters will be schmoozing" by night. Perhaps to combat (but also to feed) this elitist image, TED offers recordings of all of its talks for free online. The talks really are some of the best things available on the web, even with the excruciating BMW ads that top and tail them.

In 2007, the *Economist* called TED "Davos for optimists", in reference to the annual invitation-only World Economic Forum that is a regular target of anti-globalisation protestors. Ethan thinks "it's a more useful Davos. Davos is about putting very, very powerful people together in a ski resort in Switzerland and hoping that they all party. And they do. TED is really about the talks. The conversation starter's always, 'what was the best thing you've heard today?'"

Ethan is still reeling from a talk he heard at TED Global by Dr Jason Clay of the World Wide Fund for Nature (WWF). When I get home from interviewing Ethan, I watch Clay online. He does not look particularly nervous to be addressing TED's exclusive audience, and that's because he talks to the CEOs of the world's most powerful companies everyday of his life. He's travelled a long way since he met Ben Cohen, the Ben of Ben and Jerry's ice-cream, at a Grateful Dead benefit gig in the early 1980s, and encouraged the famously right-thinking duo to launch a brazil-nut flavoured ice cream intended to help preserve the rainforest. Although that venture did not have the determining effect on deforestation Clay had hoped, he's been honing his market intervention skills ever since. He now carries in his pocket a list of the 100 companies that, together, control around a quarter of the 15 most environmentally damaging commodities markets across the globe.

Clay's argument is simple. If you want to save the planet, what is the best way to spend your time? Is it in attempting to convince 6.9 billion consumers to buy more ethical products? Or 1.5 billion commodity producers to produce more ethical commodities (palm oil, cotton, shrimp)? Or do you go to these hundred or so mega-corps, the intermediaries that turn raw commodities into consumer goods, and convince them that it is in their long-term interests to ensure the viability of the planet they do business in? Biodiversity, ethical production, is a "pre-competitive issue", Clay says. Even if you don't like the fact that there are only a hundred of these determining mega-corps, when it comes to saving the planet, it's pretty useful they're there.

"It's really funny," says Ethan, "because it sounds like it's this giant corporate sell-out. 'I'm an environmentalist for the WWF', 'What do you do?' 'I spend my days negotiating with Cargill. I'm trying to get them to build palm trees twice as close together to get more efficient production of palm oil.'" But Ethan can see the parallels between Clay's techniques and using the rapidly consolidating web to protect free speech.

"Currently, the way we try and circumvent internet censorship is phenomenally stupid," he says. Most circumvention techniques are based around web proxies: decoy destinations set up on a volunteer or occasionally commercial (ad-supported) basis. Proxies grant safe passage to people trying to travel to parts of the web blocked by their own governments by making it look like the innocuous proxy server was their intended destination, all the while squirreling them out of the back door to the place they really wanted to go. Although effective, Ethan says this method of circumventing censorship is incredibly expensive, in much the same way that negotiating with 6.9 billion consumers to buy ethically sourced palm-oil products is incredibly expensive.

"I think that certain of our cyber-Utopian assumptions and values serve us somewhat ill in the internet today," he says, "If the internet were the internet we thought it was, with millions and millions of independent end points, then the notion of working with a single end point to end censorship would be crazy. But it's not. YouTube is a measurable and probably double-digit percent of traffic blocked in a given country. It makes a whole lot more sense to go to YouTube than it does to go to every single blocked user to fix the problem."

Trying to run a web proxy to get YouTube to users whose government blocks it, then, is the equivalent of starting your own internet service provider to provide bandwidth to a customer who doesn't pay you. "It's crazy, it's just madness. Oh and by the way it's exactly the same sort of romantic madness that we've been talking about here. That I, an independent individual on the internet, I can change the world. I'll start an anti-censorship thing. Fine, you can start an anti-censorship thing for a couple hundred, a couple thousand people. If you are phenomenally good at what you do, some tens of thousands. But are you going to get China access to YouTube? No. Fucking. Way. You just can't do it. YouTube needs to do it."

Ethan says the reason YouTube doesn't do it is because they can't make any money from it. "The problem with internet freedom is that it's not profitable to provide free access to Internet services, period. I think this is where it gets really hard for this cyber-Utopian argument. This very much started out as people committed to a vision. Doing the right thing and so on and so forth. I think Google, from this point, is committed to doing the right thing within the constraint that they're a publicly traded company that needs to do the right thing in a way that doesn't get it arrested by any number of different regulators within the US. So I'm inspired by Jason Clay. I would now like to find a way to get Google on my side by convincing them that this is good business practice and if not profitable, then at least not cripplingly unsustainable to do."

It's hardly radical – at least, it's not my kind of radical. It's not the kind of radical that smokes cigarettes in squatted factory buildings plotting revolutions, or takes to the streets in glorious technicolour. It's not glamorous, and it's not easy. It doesn't smash the system, it is the system. It is consumer politics, not citizen politics. It is corporate social responsibility. It is public relations.

But then, if it is also a good solution to a pressing problem, what kind of hacker would I be to ignore it?

chapter 8

ciphers and doppelgangers

Chapter 8: Ciphers and Doppelgangers

When I spoke to him at the Frontline Club, Ethan told me that, for now at least, he was hopeful for the US State Department's internet freedom agenda. He knew the people who wrote Hilary Clinton's January speech. "They're friends," he told me, "and they're generally not from the part of the State Department that is trying to figure out, you know, how to overthrow this government or that.

"My assumption is that Clinton says she wants the internet to be free, open and accessible because she believes it's a force for democratic good. As opposed to, say, wanting the internet everywhere because it's a great way to spread American hegemony, soft power, and start colour revolutions around the world."

Nonetheless, the new policy isn't entirely unproblematic for Ethan. Through his involvement with Global Voices, Ethan has met digital activists from all over the world, including those agitating for democratic reform in autocratic Arab states that are key US allies. One of them is Sami Ben Gharbia, an exiled Tunisian and vocal critic of the State Department policy. Several weeks after I spoke with Ethan, Sami publicly labelled Hilary Clinton's internet freedom agenda a "crusade", a word that, seven centuries after the actual Crusades took place, is still deeply politically charged in the context of Middle East politics. As oil politics slicks onto the 'net, Sami's concerns were that fragile ties made between US hackers working on anti-censorship technology and Arab digital activists making use of that technology would come under strain. Latent anti-Americanism would be fed by the hypocrisy of strategic State Department support for digital activism – helping dissidents in, say, Iran, while avoiding any action that would, as Sami wrote, "endanger the 'stability' of the dictatorial Arab order".

It's depressing to think that John Perry Barlow's "civilisation of mind" could revert so easily to nationalist lines at the first sign of trouble. When I spoke to him, Ethan was clearly torn. He could see where Sami was coming from ("There are a lot of parts of the world," he said, "where working with the US is a good way to get killed"), and yet he has a lot of expertise to offer the US State Department if they are seriously interested in helping people in repressive regimes use digital technology to speak out and organise. At the heart of every hacker is the desire to share knowledge and expertise. "I haven't got an answer to Sami. The only answer is to be wholly oppositional, where we sort of say, 'we're going to critique but we can't talk to you about what you could do better because if we talk to you then we're part of your agenda'. I just... I can't do that."

It gets messy quite quickly, but not in the way Sami expected. In September, triggered by a post by Evgeny Morozov on *Foreign Policy* magazine's Net Effect blog, question marks begin to appear around a surveillance circumvention tool called Haystack being developed with the blessing of the US State Department. Is it really doing what it says it does?

As its name suggests, Haystack deals in steganography - it purports to give users in repressive regimes the ability to mask their online behaviour, by encrypting their web traffic so it can't be intercepted, then hiding it like a needle in a haystack of made-up, unencrypted junk traffic to make sure no-one notices the encryption. It's a clever response to traffic profiling. The surveillance authorities know that a proportion of everybody's web traffic will be encrypted – when they make financial transactions online, for example. But if your traffic profile includes much more encrypted traffic than the average person, then in the mind of the Iranian cyber-snoop, that means you must have something to hide.

But nobody outside of the Censorship Research Center (CRC), the corporate body set up to support the Haystack software and process funding, has actually seen how it works. This is highly unusual for this kind of software. As Rop told me at CCC, the debate about the best way to make sure software is secure was over by the mid-nineties. Disclosure is the only way to make sure a piece of software is secure. Security through obscurity – the principle Haystack used to hide its code from public view when it argued that disclosure would put the lives of Haystack's Iranian user base in peril – doesn't cut it. Bruce Schneier famously puts it this way: "Anyone can invent a security system that he himself cannot break."

Haystack hadn't shown their code to anyone, having developed it for the most part outside of the traditional cyber-security and censorship-circumvention tools community. In fact, Haystack wasn't like any previous censorship and surveillance circumvention tool in lots of ways, including the fact it had a frontman who, although unwilling to share his code with anyone, was very willing to talk to the international press about why it was so great.

That man was the charismatic Austin Heap, a good-looking 25-year-old San Francisco marketing graduate described as a "computer savant" in one of the many beatifying profiles that followed the launch of Haystack into the public consciousness. In the six months before Evgeny Morozov sounded the alarm, Austin happily posed for the camera bound and gagged by network cables, bragging about the many appointments with State Department officials crowding out his schedule, and accepting the awed curiosity of journalists with mock humility. If you were paying any attention to this sort of thing, you probably saw Heap yourself in a lifestyle magazine, blog or tech supplement during this period. I met him briefly in March, when we sat on a panel together at an event hosted by the *Guardian*. He was late, so I didn't get a chance to speak to him much before the event. Afterwards he was mobbed by a gaggle of young female groupies. A friend and I looked on, amused and slightly jealous at the rockstar status of digital rights campaigners these days.

Austin had swagger, much of it learned from the older hacker communities that hang out at places like CCC. And Austin was all too ready to give the newspapers what they wanted, trading on the usually unarticulated threat of the lone and highly-skilled hacker, like some kind of doppelganger to Julian Assange. "We will systematically take on each repressive country that censors its people," he told *Newsweek* in August, "We have a list. Don't piss off hackers who will have their way with you. A mischievous kid will show you how the Internet works."

But as it turned out, he didn't have the skills to back up his claims. Though he purported to deal in cryptography, Austin turned out to be nothing but a cipher himself. After Evgeny's piece for *Foreign Policy*, the code fell into the hands of Jacob Appelbaum, a hacker of considerable pedigree who had spoken on behalf of WikiLeaks at a US conference in July while Julian was in hiding (and who, for his troubles, was subsequently detained at the airport the next time he flew into the US). Appelbaum's verdict was unequivocal, delivered via Twitter on 14 September: "Haystack is the worst piece of software I have ever had the displeasure of ripping apart. Charlatans exposed. Media inquiries welcome."

The fallout was swift and punishing. The CRC Board of directors resigned en bloc, as did Haystack's only developer Dan Colascione. The Electronic Frontier Foundation issued a short statement urging anybody testing Haystack in Iran to stop using the product immediately, for their own safety. A few days later, Heap too stepped down from his position as Executive Director. During the fallout, I spoke to one insider who said that she was worried that given the youthful naivety of many of the players involved, the next piece of news could well be a suicide.

Danny O'Brien, a prominent digital rights campaigner who was in the room while Jake Appelbaum put Haystack through its paces, captured his reaction to the news that the software was a fraud:

> Coders and architects need to realize (as most do) that you simply can't build a safe, secure, reliable system without consulting with other people in the field, especially when your real adversary is a powerful and resourceful state-sized actor, and this is your first major project.

Evgeny Morozov was less kind. As well as calling out the State Department and the media for letting Haystack overhype itself for so long, he mused that the Haystack scenario revealed "the timidity of the current debate in the field". He named Ethan and several of his colleagues at Berkman, berating them for avoiding confrontation with the State Department. "The tough and probably inevitable dilemma," Morozov concluded, "is between helping the government get it right and helping the public get it right, by being in a strong position to criticize the government".

chapter
9
infowar

Chapter 9: Infowar

Pinned on the notice board on the wall of my office is a document I will eventually frame. It is two pages of A4 bearing my signature, alongside the autograph of, at the time, the most wanted man in the world. It is titled simply "WikiLeaks Confidentiality Agreement".

Here's what happened.

About halfway through October, I received a text from a friend from the campaign trail asking me if I was in London and, if so, whether I wanted to help do some good in the world. Curious, and by chance in the capital, I texted back. Less than a minute later my friend calls to ask if I would like to speak to "our mutual friend". Our mutual friend turns out to be Julian Assange.

Julian doesn't want to talk much on the phone, so we arrange to meet later that day, at (where else?) the Frontline Club. As

I get through the day's appointments, I find myself increasingly concerned about what is in store for me later at Frontline. A lot has happened since the release of the Afghan War Logs. Back in June, Rop wrote a blog post distancing himself from the WikiLeaks operation, an act that on the face of things looked simply like an attempt to rid himself of nuisance calls from an increasingly curious global press, but could well have hidden deeper disagreements. Then in August Swedish prosecutors publicly opened an investigation into Assange's behaviour towards two Swedish women, both of whom claimed to have been sexually assaulted by him. In September Julian's co-spokesperson at WikiLeaks, Daniel Schmitt, whose real name turned out to be Daniel Domscheit-Berg, publicly quit WikiLeaks citing irreconcilable differences with its "emperor" leader Assange.

I decide to call Rop Gonggrijp to see if he can tell me whether WikiLeaks is still a good organisation to work with. I don't expect Rop to still have my number in his phone, so when he answers my call with a friendly and welcoming "Hello Becky," I'm pleased. I quickly explain my unexpected call, and ask if Julian is still in the circle of trust. Which, apparently, he is.

"So why did you stop working with him?" I ask.

"It turns out I don't have the right constitution, I couldn't cope with the excitement," says Rop.

I'm not sure I have the right constitution either, but what harm can a meeting do? I resolve to go. Before he lets me hang up, Rop asks me, with a soft reprimand in his voice, how I am.

"And how is the book going?" he asks.

I tell him I'll send it to him, and we arrange to meet in Amsterdam in December to discuss all that has happened since Chaos.

Julian arrives at the Frontline bar just under half an hour after our arranged meeting time. The plan is to go straight to the new WikiLeaks bunker, down the road above the offices of the Frontline Trust. But as we are halfway out of the door, Julian spots the G&T I'm clutching and has a change of heart. We turn back and order him one, and the barman confirms that now we both have the drinks, the only honourable thing would be for us to stay and drink them where we are. Julian doesn't seem to mind – in fact, he looks relieved to take a break.

Julian remembers me from Chaos, and remembers he had a terrible cough when we spoke – something I'd forgotten, but which explains the etiolated impression he made on me then. He's looking much healthier now, buoyant, even. I'm clutching the first draft of this book. As I fan the pages at him in mock pride, I realise how often his name appears on them. Since we met, the figure of his public persona, as constructed by hundreds of news reporters, bloggers and commentators across the world, has overwhelmed the figure of the quiet, determined man I spent time with in Berlin. Now I have him back in front of me, I feel like I'm being visited by a ghost.

Nonetheless, the conversation flows freely. We talk about Daniel Domscheit-Berg, about the Swedish legal system, about recent secret trade negotiations to strengthen the intellectual property enforcement framework. We talk about what it feels like to be pursued by the international news media. Pretty soon, we're heading over to the new bunker.

The first thing that surprises me when we get there is the haircut. A man with an enormous quiff, dressed in full East London psychobilly, is running the room. I get the feeling I had at c-Base, or when I saw Austin Heap surrounded by groupies in March: these people are too trendy to be into computers. Introductions made, contracts signed, Julian steals me into the kitchen to talk about what he's doing and how I can help.

He tells me everything he's planning. On 23 October, the day the confidentiality agreement I've just signed runs out, a number of newspapers and broadcasters from across the world who've signed agreements like my one – including Al-Jazeera – will begin publishing the Iraq War Logs. Both in their number, and in what they reveal, they will dwarf the Afghan logs. The Iraq logs will reveal US complicity in the torture of hundreds of Iraqis. They will reveal a civilian death toll bigger even than the one currently being maintained by the humanitarian research group Iraq Body Count. And they will hit the press just over a week before the United States mid-term elections.

Julian talks rapidly, and doesn't welcome interruption. Although what he is saying sounds reasonable, his tendency to ascribe the various difficulties that have beset WikiLeaks to conspiracy is noticeable. For example, according to Julian, statements made by Reporters Without Borders and Amnesty International condemning the Afghan War Logs for revealing the names of informants were engineered by forces in Washington, who targeted soft people within each group to get the statements out. I find it easier to believe that these organisations were confused by WikiLeaks' strategy, genuinely concerned for the safety of Afghans, and unwilling to bet their hard-won reputations on a free speech gamble they didn't fully understand.

Nonetheless, WikiLeaks is learning from experience. Julian tells me that, as with the newspapers, this time around he has also reached out in advance to NGOs like the ones that condemned the Afghan release, and they're on side. On the day of the release, the plan is for WikiLeaks to hold a news conference alongside Iraq Body Count and the law firm Public Interest Lawyers, who are currently representing Iraqis claiming to have been victims of torture at the hands of UK forces. The strategy will do a lot to contextualise the leaked documents, to keep the focus on what the material reveals and away from Julian and WikiLeaks. Now, alongside the military talking heads that so swiftly talked down the Afghan War Logs, there will be dedicated human rights campaigners, pushing another message.

Julian is looking for volunteers to help run a press room on the day of the release. But I want to know why. Why does WikiLeaks even need to be at the news conference? Hasn't Julian learned from the past that he and his organisation merely serve to distract from the material they release? If they returned to the shadows the day after the release, wouldn't that cut off the oxygen supply of a popular press bent on making a story of human rights abuses turn into a story about one blonde Australian? Julian tells me they need to be there to contextualise the material, to make sure that it gets reported beyond a few headline-grabbing documents. But that can't be why, I counter, because the evidence should have shown him by now that things won't play out that way. What's the real reason?

It turns out it's about credit. WikiLeaks needs to be there, says Julian, so that credit gets to the right people.

I find this odd. I remind him of a quote that a mutual friend of ours – the security expert Ben Laurie – uses to sign off every email: "There is no limit to what a man can do or how far he can go if he doesn't mind who gets the credit". Apparently it was said by Robert Woodruff, the President of the Coca Cola corporation between 1923 and 1954. Julian knows the sign-off well.

"But it turns out," he says, "that Ben's wrong."

Just as Julian planned it, on 23 October, the Iraq War Logs release begins. According to *Der Spiegel*, who along with the *Guardian*, the *New York Times*, and newbies Al Jazeera and *Le Monde* enjoyed embargoed access to the material in the weeks leading up to the release, it is the biggest leak in the military history of the United States. Iraq Body Count, who have also had the material for some time, declare that it shows 15,000 more civilian deaths than previously counted, meaning that of all the people killed during the Iraq conflict, four in every five of them was a civilian. More shocking still, the material reveals how US forces handed over prisoners of war to Iraqi authorities knowing they would be subjected to torture, an action that Amnesty International quickly point out is illegal under international law.

The *New York Times* attracts criticism for its coverage. Instead of headlining the US complicity in torture, it places these revelations beneath stories about failed strategy and tactics, and phrases the eventual stories on civilian deaths and torture in language that looks very much like it has been sanitised by the Pentagon. The paper also includes a damning profile of Julian in its front page coverage, entitled "WikiLeaks Founder on the Run, Trailed by Notoriety". The article draws on criticisms from Daniel Domscheit-Berg and some Icelandic volunteers no longer working with WikiLeaks, as well as a conversation with Julian that sounds remarkably similar to the one I had, to paint a picture of a paranoid despot on the edge of reason, and on the run.

The leaks now go into warp drive. On the Sunday after Thanksgiving, some of the same news outlets begin publishing selected US diplomatic cables from a corpus WikiLeaks says numbers over a quarter of a million and dates back to 1966. The first 260, published on 28 November, reveal instructions to US diplomats to gather information about UN officials which the *Guardian* describe as "blur[ring] the line between diplomacy and spying", as well as historic cables about the release of Nelson Mandela in 1990 and a number of cables from around the Middle East that have to do with Iran, its nuclear programme, and the 2009 Iranian elections. The days that follow feature tittle-tattle with high entertainment value (Prince Andrew acting like a tit in his role as special trade representative; US diplomats across the world making snarky comments about national leaders) mixed in with the odd serious revelation about corruption and extra-judicial killing in Pakistan, or China's weakening diplomatic stance over North Korea. The press call it Cablegate.

But something about this fresh set of leaks is different. This time, for the first time, WikiLeaks doesn't simultaneously publish the entire corpus on its own website, only the cables selected by its newspaper partners, effectively giving the mainstream media a permanent scoop. Why? Most likely, given WikiLeaks' dwindling resources and the quick turnaround of Cablegate following the Iraq War Logs, they simply didn't have time to do the necessary redactions. But what was influencing the timing? Why did they have to release the cables so quickly after the Iraq War Logs?

Perhaps Julian knew his time was running out. A week after the first Cablegate stories came out, Scotland Yard let Julian know that they had received a European Arrest Warrant from Swedish prosecutors investigating the allegations of sexual assault made against him in the summer, and they were planning to act on it. The next morning, on 7 December, he was arrested by appointment at a London police station. At a hearing that afternoon, Julian was refused bail and sent to Wandsworth prison.

Back in May, when I was talking to Ethan at the Frontline Club about pseudo-public spaces, about the dangers of seeing virtual town squares where only virtual shopping malls exist, it all seemed so abstract. Well thanks to WikiLeaks, in early December, it got a whole lot less abstract.

Most people know Amazon as the world's biggest online retailer. But since about 2007 it has been hawking something altogether different to the tech-savvy hacker - machines. Amazon's S3 cloud computing service is used by most hardcore data geeks I know as a quick and easy way to add more computing power to their programs, services and experiments. As it happened, in December WikiLeaks were also using Amazon's S3 service, a fact that did not go unnoticed by the US authorities. On 30 November, Senator Joe Lieberman had a quiet word with Amazon. On 1 December, the website was taken offline.

Amazon's official line was that WikiLeaks had violated its Terms of Service by publishing information (the cables) to which it didn't own the rights. WikiLeaks was violating copyright, Amazon said. It didn't matter that this argument was obvious bullshit (in the US, it is a constitutional prerogative that nobody can claim ownership of information produced by the government). Because Amazon is a commercial company and not a democratically elected government, it can more or less pick and choose with whom it does business. Like most internet companies with any sense it had designed its Terms of Service to be baggy enough to let it make those decisions. And after a little conversation with Joe Lieberman, Amazon had decided it didn't want to do business with WikiLeaks.

Just as Bluehost had with Zimbabwean activists Kubatana, Amazon had made the obvious business decision that, no matter what the legal niceties, WikiLeaks were not worth the trouble. But what was WikiLeaks doing hosting with a US-based mega-provider like Amazon in the first place? Surely they had the smarts to run their own operation?

The truth is that since the day before the Cablegate leaks, WikiLeaks had been subjected to cyber-attacks called "Distributed Denial of Service", or DDoS. DDoS attacks route tons of bogus traffic to a website's servers, creating jams that stop legitimate traffic from getting through and effectively taking the website offline. There is no easy solution to these sorts of attacks, and DDoS attacks are the most expensive issue facing network operators across the web. Major websites, like Google, or CNN.com, invest in serious resources to mitigate the effects of attacks – complex filtering techniques to identify the bogus traffic, or banks of redundant servers that effectively widen the road until all the traffic can get through. Although these websites may be under constant DDoS attack, their users generally don't notice – thanks to the expensive techniques their operators apply, they can still get through.

The DDoS attacks, which were claimed by a pro-US hacker calling himself "The Jester", were more than WikiLeaks could cope with on their own. Moving to Amazon meant they could increase the supply of servers and bandwidth to meet the demands of all the traffic coming their way – bogus or otherwise. But it also meant that they were putting their mission in the hands of a giant American corporate. And on 1 December, that giant American corporate washed its hands of their mission.

Coincidentally, as part of his work for the Berkman Center, Ethan Zuckerman was just polishing off a report on DDoS attacks and their effect on independent media and human rights websites when the news about Amazon and WikiLeaks broke. "It's the sort of in-depth, detailed work we do at Berkman," he wrote on his blog, "that we generally expect to be of interest to the folks who funded the research and to a small group of people whose work focuses on protecting human rights and independent media sites from DDoS attack." For the past year, Ethan and his colleagues had been working with independent media and human rights groups in Russia, China, Iran, Kazakhstan, Uzbekistan, Egypt, Tunisia, Vietnam and Burma, trying to get a sense of how often DDoS was being used as an instrument to suppress free speech. They had come to the conclusion that not only was it an increasingly common form of attack, it was a form of attack that was impossible for these small-scale individual operations to prevent. As a result, one of the report's major recommendations was to encourage independent media and human rights organisations to host their websites closer to the "core" of the network – at hypergiant providers like Amazon and Google – in order to take advantage of their expertise and resources when it came to fending off DDoS. Amazon's actions against WikiLeaks had "complicated" that conclusion, Ethan wrote.

Stuck between exposure to crippling cyber-attacks at the edge of the network, and the risk of political pressure and censorship at the network's core, it looked like the real world was closing in on WikiLeaks. What's more, amid rumours of pressure from the highest ranks of the US State Department, first PayPal, then Mastercard and Visa choked WikiLeaks' ability to receive donations, refusing to process any more payments destined for WikiLeaks and, in PayPal's case, cutting off access to their account. But if extra-judicial censorship of WikiLeaks was as easy as a few phone calls from the powers-that-be, it was also about to turn out to be impossible.

On 3 December, techno-Utopian and WELL original John Perry Barlow posted the following on Twitter:

> The first serious infowar is now engaged. The field of battle is WikiLeaks. You are the troops.

It was 14 years since his Declaration of Independence, and it was time to fight for Cyberspace.

And so the internet struck back. In the days that followed hundreds, and then thousands of so-called "mirror" sites sprang up across the web, all publishing the information that Joe Lieberman had sought to suppress. And because the mainstream media weren't about to stop highlighting the cables – free speech being at least a little more central to the *New York Times'* business model than it is to Amazon's – attention to the content of the cables continued to increase. Trapped in this hall of mirrors, distorted reflections of their diplomatic activity would haunt the US State Department with every step it took.

A loosely-affiliated group of individuals calling themselves Anonymous also sprung into action. This relatively anarchic spectre of an organisation had previously rallied itself against geek-friendly targets such as the various lobby groups representing Hollywood film studios and major record labels. Now it turned its attention to Amazon, Paypal, Visa and Mastercard. It asked those outraged by these companies' actions to download a piece of software that enabled them to join a voluntary botnet, controlled by Anonymous. This virtual army of machines then invaded target websites in its own series of DDoS attacks. Predictably, Amazon was able to sustain the attacks. But the homepages of Paypal, Visa and Mastercard were successfully taken down, and there were even reports of trouble processing credit card payments – a worrying development for online retailers at the height of the Christmas shopping period.

And so, as Julian Assange prepared for his first night's stay at Her Majesty's pleasure in Wandsworth Prison, he did so knowing the world outside might be slowly collapsing under the weight of what he had helped WikiLeaks to achieve. And I can't help hoping that he slept soundly.

The day that followed Julian's arrest, I was in Amsterdam heading for Rop's house.

The journey had not been planned to coincide with Julian's incarceration, but rather with a trip to Brussels I was making anyway. I had spent the previous evening at the Frontline Club, ready to catch the Eurostar first thing the following day. Across the bar from where I sat I had seen WikiLeaks volunteers and supporters commiserating the judge's decision not to grant Julian bail. One I'd spoken to feared he would never again see Julian alive. By coincidence, I had arranged to dine with Ben Laurie, my friend and also one of the few people associated early on with WikiLeaks as a security advisor. Ben's phone had not stopped ringing all day, a global media stampede that had left Ben feeling bruised and harassed. I wondered if Rop was in a similar state.

It was early evening, and snow lay thick on the ground of the smart suburban street where Rop lives with his family. Snow and also ice, making any kind of quick progress down the long row of tall houses next to impossible. At that moment this was a problem since on top of my bags, I was clutching a bottle of red wine. As my shoes zig-zagged on the ice, I had visions of it crashing to the pavement, blood-red liquid seeping through the snow like a Slush Puppie. I didn't even know if Rop drank wine. I was nervous and I needed to calm down.

Outside of the UK vernaculars, I know next to nothing about architecture, but when abroad I do take with me the Englishman's sense for the property ladder. Looking at the buildings around me, I guessed we were quite near the top, a sort of Dutch Notting Hill. The fact that on the tram ride here I had passed large billboards advertising Rop's old business, XS4ALL, was of course a clue that I wasn't about to be headed anywhere too scruffy. So when finally I arrived at Rop's number, I was surprised to see a row of doorbells next to it indicating the building had been split into apartments. A closer inspection revealed, however, that they all said "Gonggrijp". I pressed one at random.

Back in 2005, at the 22nd annual Chaos Communication Congress (22c3) Rop gave a talk called *We Lost the War*. The talk, which he delivered together with Chaos Computer Club spokesperson Frank Rieger, was controversial both within and beyond the hacker community. Ostensibly, it was about privacy. Privacy-conscious hackers, Rieger and Gongrijjp argued, had not kept pace with technological development. Too many of them had gone to work for the dark side, creating the very tools they should be guarding against. The surveillance capabilities already here or about to come online – from vast, permanent databases of number plate records gathered from roads across the Western world, to data mining and behaviour-predicting algorithms and facial recognition technology – were Erich Honecker's "wet dream". And thanks to 9/11, new laws were being passed – most notably the EU's Data Retention Directive – that gave the authorities blanket powers to store and manipulate surveillance information in whatever way they wanted.

This was not all. Several external forces – globalisation, climate change, and the resource wars and mass migration that would inevitably follow – were creating the conditions for a "perfect storm". Soon, every citizen would be a potential threat, an enemy of state stability. Powers reserved for combating terrorism would be unleashed on the entire population.

Against such an irresistible force, what could hackers have done differently? They had lost, just as they were always going to.

You can still watch videos of this talk online. As he delivers the bad news, Rop speaks in a monotone. He looks as depressed as his talk is depressing, and he sounds like he has given up. My initial reason for wanting to speak to Rop again, for organising this trip, was to ask him, what had got him through it? How can you make a statement like the "We Lost the War" speech, and then get up and carry on fighting?

But now, as I waited for Rop to let me into his house, I had other things on my mind. I wasn't seeking inspiration, I was seeking shelter. That day, I didn't feel part of the world. The entire globe was talking about Julian Assange, and I didn't want to listen anymore. I felt implicated. I felt scared, I felt ashamed.

And I felt like the only person I could talk to about it was Rop. When he answered the door, we gave each other a big hug.

"I'm no Julian," says Rop. "There's a level beyond which I start worrying about very mundane things, like the fact that I need to be with my kids and raise them. And about where I'm going to live. I can't be living out of a backpack from airport to airport."

We're sitting in Rop's basement office the afternoon after my arrival, and he's telling me why he stopped helping WikiLeaks. In the weeks and months that followed his trip to Washington from Reykjavik to release the *Collateral Murder* video, as he began to have time to think on his own again, it slowly dawned on him what he had become involved in. He calls it a "primal fear", a "fight or flight reflex". He doesn't want to make excuses for his decision to abandon WikiLeaks, to blame made-up disagreements, he says, or to make himself out as an independent thinker who just couldn't stomach Julian's leadership style, although he admits that he could see Julian might have started getting to him if their collaboration had lasted longer.

No. Put simply, he says, it "scared the motherfucking bejesus out of me".

It's important to know that Rop isn't a man who is easily scared. In 1996 the internet service provider he founded, XS4ALL, became the target of an aggressive copyright lawsuit brought by the Church of Scientology. The litigation was to continue for nearly a decade, and would define subsequent national and European laws passed to regulate and protect internet service providers like XS4ALL.

It all started when one of XS4ALL's customers had used his homepage to post a confidential set of course materials produced by the Church, called the Operating Thetan documents.

"Scientology wasn't happy about having all of these documents online," says Rop. "And that's an understatement. They were very, very unhappy."

Scientology sued XS4ALL for copyright infringement. It was a mismatched fight, explains Rop, as the Church's legal resources far outstripped their own. But working together with Dutch free speech advocate Karin Spaink, XS4ALL stood their ground. The case reached the Dutch Supreme Court and could have gone all the way to Europe had the Church of Scientology not finally withdrawn in it 2005. On the way, the controversy established several key ideas about how companies like XS4ALL should operate online, what regulations should bind them, and what activities they should not be held liable for. Rop characterises it as one of the first fights about the freedom of the internet.

"Our argument was that our service was no different from what the phone company does. You can't sue them for the stuff people say over the phone. Or that this was just somebody renting a house from us and putting a poster in their window. If you have a problem with that person, go to court. If a judge orders us to do something, we'll happily do it. But we're no party in this." That point of view is now enshrined in European and US law.

In the US, this legislation is called the Digital Millennium Copyright Act, and in Europe, it's called the E-Commerce Directive, which will give you some idea of the kind of arguments that won the legislators round when it came to drafting it. Both laws grant online service providers like XS4ALL – and, incidentally, Amazon's S3 cloud hosting service – immunity from prosecution for copyright infringement at least until they receive an official notification that they are hosting potentially infringing content. And note that in this context, an official notification isn't the same thing as a friendly telephone call from Senator Joe Lieberman.

If legislators hadn't exempted providers from liability in this way, the world wide web could have never grown to the size it is today. But nothing in these laws compels services like Amazon S3 to host content. Now, with Amazon's decision to take down WikiLeaks seemingly on corporate whim, we are facing the opposite situation. Should providers benefitting from common carrier status be compelled to host content their paying customers ask them to, until some kind of judicial order compels them not to? Or is that a crazy idea?

Rop pauses for a moment. "I guess in principle," he eventually replies, "I support Amazon's right to take the decision they did. As long as there is enough competition. As long as there is viable competition I think I would support the right of an ISP not to host stuff. That said, this only goes until there's a virtual monopoly. At which point you have no freedom of speech anymore. And we're seeing the development of a number of virtual monopolies in the space of communication. I think Facebook is a particularly evil monopoly. Because it's like the phonebook.

You can't be in a different phonebook because people only look in one phonebook. So I'm hoping for Facebook to be replaced by something de-central, something which uses Facebook, which morphs into Facebook but isn't Facebook. And there are a number of new initiatives in this space."

The hacker's answer – if you don't like something, then build something better. In a few weeks, Rop and I will be at CCC. Most people there with us will know where they can host material if they're afraid that a mainstream provider will take it down. They'll know how they can communicate with their networks such that the government can't eavesdrop on them. But the fact that hackers can protect themselves won't be that useful to mainstream society. They'll be a minority. Most of the world will be on the corporate web, the Murdoch web, where virtual speech is even more circumscribed, perhaps, than it is in the real world. Isn't that a major problem?

"I'm just wondering whether that's ever been different", says Rop. "I mean, if you had information that wasn't in the mainstream press in the eighties, you would need to stencilate, or get it out on pirate radio, or get it in certain bookstores that would sell it. There was a circuit for information that wasn't desirable to the powers that be or to the mainstream media. And that circuit is still the reality now. It's just grown immensely."

According to Rop, then, the technologies routinely used by the hacker community – decentralised communications systems, encryption, steganography – may never break into the mainstream. Facebook and YouTube will be the internet for the rest of us. But if the medium stays buried underground, that doesn't necessarily mean that the message will too. Perhaps – so long as these technologies are not completely eradicated, so long as information can be free across at least one portion of the network – the hacker community, like radical movements before it, could act as a stalking horse for more mainstream political discourse?

In fact, isn't that what WikiLeaks is doing right now?

Since I arrived in his home, Rop and I have talked on and off about how we feel about Julian, and about how he feels about the decision he took to pull out while he still could. Rop is pretty sure there's a whiteboard in Washington with his name on it. As a hacker and long-time campaigner, he's used to being of interest to the security services. But although he's not particularly bothered by the idea of Dutch spooks taking an interest in him, US spooks are a difference matter. Rop's noticed that he now gets great mobile reception in his basement.

Last night Rop and I searched for pictures of Wandsworth Prison. When I first interviewed Rop back at 26c3, I hadn't realised what good friends he and Julian had become. After they'd both spoken at a conference in Kuala Lumpur in October 2009, they'd spent a month travelling together around Malaysia, Thailand and Cambodia.

"I don't think I have a guilt complex," he tells me, "I don't think I'm concerned that he's in prison and I'm not. I think Julian long ago made choices in his life that I can't make. Living in airports, being on the run. But that's also something that he's cultivated. I've travelled with Julian and know that creature comforts are just something that's not important to him. He'll miss being online, being able to talk to people. But he does not care about where he sleeps. I've seen him sleep in chairs at airports, in a hallway against the wall. I don't think British prisons have a level of discomfort which he would even notice."

Julian isn't the only person Rop's worked with this year who has ended up in prison. In between his trips to Iceland, Rop had been visiting India to speak about the perils of computer-mediated voting at conferences and to meet with Indian politicians. At 714 million, India has the world's largest electorate, and votes in its elections are cast almost exclusively on electronic voting machines. In April, together with several other researchers, Rop published a paper which demonstrated two serious vulnerabilities in the electronic voting machines used in these elections, machines to which he had had access on one of his visits. The following August, Hari Prasad, a security researcher from Hyderabad, was arrested and, after refusing to disclose the source of the machine they had tested together, thrown in gaol.

At the time, Rop wrote on his blog:

> All of this makes me pause at the fact in some countries the truth has a much longer road to travel and that people in those countries are exposed to some very real personal risks for speaking out.

Thankfully, Hari was released a week later, after organisations including the Electronic Frontier Foundation highlighted his case to the world.

Rop tells me what happened. "Until now, the Election Commission of India have always claimed that the voting machines were perfect, immaculate, completely untamperable. Any rumour that they were tamperable was spread by evil people that had no clue. And we just took the machine and we proved that, just like with any other black box voting machine, if you have time to study it a little bit and then have momentary access to a machine afterwards, you can do anything you want. A black box voting machine can be programmed to count the votes honestly. It can just as well be programmed to count the votes dishonestly. Or even play chess."

Programming a voting machine to play chess might seem like an odd thing to do, but in 2006, that's exactly what Rop did here in the Netherlands, with a voting machine manufactured by a company called Nedap.

Rop had been campaigning against the use of computers in Dutch municipal elections for some time. Nedap were less than keen on sharing their schematics and code with Rop and his fellow campaigners, and just as Austin Heap's refusal to submit the Haystack code for review had raised suspicions among the wider security community, the Dutch e-voting campaigners didn't think this could be right. Nedap claimed that the way the machines worked was a trade secret, an assertion Rop thought was ridiculous. The way an election works needs to be transparent to the entire electorate, or else, how can they accept the results? This isn't just a technical issue. It's telling that, when ORG was campaigning against e-voting, the political party that followed our campaign the closest was the BNP. If you can't convince enough people to vote for you, the next best thing to do is to convince the people who do support you that the election is rigged, using whatever seed of doubt you have available to sow. That's why the fairly stable democracies that make up the Organisation for Security and Co-operation in Europe (OSCE) send international observers to make official statements on the conduct of elections in more unstable democracies. If failed oppositions seed doubts as to whether results are legitimate, post-election violence can soon escalate.

Rop had yet to get hold of a Nedap machine to test out his theory that it was vulnerable to hacking when he made a public statement that he could probably teach the voting machine to play chess. The response from Nedap was patronising enough that when he did get hold of one, it was the first thing he wanted to do.

"They said something to the effect of 'No, no, no, chess? On our voting machine? That's not possible. Here we can really see that these hackers are a little bit crazy.' So the first thing we did even before making it count the votes dishonestly, just to make sure we understood how it worked, was make it play chess. That was actually quite difficult because it had so little memory. In the end, it played quite crappy chess."

But it still played chess, and, more importantly, could be made to count votes dishonestly. Rop also found other voting machines that were being used in Dutch elections that broadcast what voters were voting – something even he did not expect. None of this was terribly good news for Nedap. The Dutch market is now closed to them. The Netherlands votes with a pencil and paper.

Rop is not anti-business, he doesn't mind private companies selling "technology" to use for elections, "whether it's paper ballots, ballot boxes, screens to put up around the ballot, pencils. The thing about that technology is that it's inert. It can only do its purpose and the mechanisms for the elections are such that even in their inert state they're actually checked. The procedures say, 'thou shall check whether the ballot box is empty.' That it's really just a simple box, it doesn't have a double bottom, that it's not some magician's device. So even those inert objects are actually checked to see whether they perform the functions that you think they will perform. There's no dependency on their storage, or their manufacture. They can be sold to you by the devil himself."

In fact, the problem Rop has encountered in his continuing campaigns against electronic voting – in 2011, he will take his campaign to Brazil – is more subtle than that, and far more sinister. He says the electorate has been "removed as a stakeholder" in the conduct of elections. He says that the election bureaucracy and the vendors see themselves as the sole stakeholders in how the election is conducted. Their major interest is expediency, and audit has become a "fail criteria", which means that demands to see how the election works means they have failed.

Democracy as theatre, democracy as service – this all reminds me of my conversation, six months ago, with Phil from No2ID. Is this the customer helpdesk model of democracy at work again? Is democracy, too, something we are supposed to consume, and not create?

When Rop gave his *We Lost the War* speech in 2005, he warned that the technologies of control and surveillance that the networked digital machines he loved to tinker with so much had brought into being would conspire with circumstance to change the face of the world. And he saw the state as the biggest danger.

"No single company getting out of control can do the amount of damage that a state getting out of control can do. And no single company has the same amount of interest in controlling the population that the state has," he says.

"But," I ask, "What's the point? What's the point of campaigning for reform when the forces against which you're campaigning can be so powerful?" I'm thinking about Julian again, and Rop knows it. He lets out a slow breath of air, which is almost a shiver.

"There are various levels of answer for that," he pauses, "I guess for me personally the point is that I wouldn't know what to do otherwise. I guess the point is that people, even in much more adversarial regimes and times, have done the same thing and that's why we're here. People have resisted the Nazi rule of this country in the 1940s under a much greater threat than Julian or Hari Prasad or anybody else has been under recently. The threat of literally being taken out and shot the same day, or tortured first. So if they dared then why shouldn't I dare? Why shouldn't anybody else dare?"

But Rop seems unsatisfied with this answer. "I'm also not sure... A lot of things that I fought for I don't think, at least in this country, have the type of opposition that is ominous and omnipresent and dangerous and evil. I don't think electronic voting in this country had an evil master plan. Or even particularly evil vendors. Yes, they were incompetent. They were selling crap and they knew it. They were colluding with local politicians who just wanted their elections to be easier and didn't worry about transparency. Which is all bad. But it's not ominous and it doesn't make you go home at night watching carefully when you cross the road.

"I think most of what we're fighting still today in the world is incompetence. Most of what we're fighting is stupidity, and maybe a little bit of opportunism. There is also the ominous, control-seeking large corporate interests. Of course that exists. You only need to read the cables to see that that exists. But mostly it's incompetence. Mostly it's opportunism. And a lot of the fights can be won. My personal quest is to look for fights that I can win."

Rop is giving this year's opening keynote at CCC. He agrees with me that most people in the audience will be thinking about WikiLeaks. Just a year ago, Julian and Daniel were the heroes of this community. Now they have split in a public and acrimonious way, and one of them is in gaol. Everything they said they would do when they spoke at 26c3 they have done, and the world has taken serious notice. How can Rop help them think things through? How can he set the right tone?

He smiles, "It freaks me out," he shouts to no-one in particular, just to get it off his chest.

I ask him what he thinks WikiLeaks set out to achieve, and whether he thinks it's succeeded.

"That's a hard one to call," he replies. "You'd have to look into Julian's brain. I think WikiLeaks set out to open governments and to raise the cost of secrecy. One can only conclude that's worked."

What does Rop think will happen now?

"That's the part of it where my thoughts on WikiLeaks are highly unfinished. I have no clue."

Could WikiLeaks actually promote a backlash, a restriction of our freedoms similar to the restrictions that were imposed after 9/11?

"Sure", says Rop, "That's not hard to imagine. But I could also imagine this leading to global reform. It's too soon to call.

"We're literally just smack in the middle of the start of it."

Epilogue
• • •

Epilogue: Return to Chaos

The 27th Chaos Communication Congress was subtitled "We Come in Peace" and for the first time, the Club sold tickets in advance. They were released in three batches, with the third and final batch selling out in around five minutes. I was lucky enough to get my hands on a ticket.

Berlin that December was minus 10°C. Snow lay thick on the ground and, like the weather, the atmosphere inside the conference was heavier too. 350 journalists had accredited to attend the event – an almost tenfold increase on last year. And it wasn't only the media who had upped their interest in the Congress. I was told by several people I met that this year's Congress was attracting better spies, too. By which I think they meant ones that blended in more.

The atmosphere was heavy, but it wasn't that heavy. If I was looking for existential angst among a community that suddenly found its values and activities in the eye of a global media storm, I was to be disappointed. Indeed, the figure of Julian Assange – now out of gaol but physically prevented from coming by the electronic tag attached to his bail conditions – was metaphorically absent as well. I spoke to one hacker who told me he thought Julian had "transferred his campaign to a different theatre of operations". By contrast, evidence of the campaign to Free Bradley Manning was everywhere.

Daniel Domscheit-Berg was there, surrounded by journalists. When I did get half an hour alone with him in the press room, his phone rang so frequently it was impossible to have a sensible conversation. He told me he couldn't keep up with the voicemails he was getting – in the week after Cablegate over 80 had been automatically deleted from his phone before he had found any time to listen to them. He looked harassed, but content. I asked him if he felt angry about what had happened. "You should have a glance on the internal mailing list of this club," he responded, "and you would know why everyone's pretty hardened about arguments".

"Free software," another person I spoke to at the conference explained, "is all about egos. Everyone here is an asshole. But we know that, and we can work with that".

Ten days earlier, a Tunisian man had set himself on fire in front of the provincial headquarters of the Tunisian government, in protest at police brutality and corruption. The desperate act was to set off a chain of uprisings across the country and then the region, that led to the overthrow of first the Tunisian and then the Egyptian governments. Libyans, concerned that their own uprising was about to be brutally suppressed by their autocratic leader Colonel Gaddafi, called on the UN for help, and a coalition of Western and Arab forces began a campaign of airstrikes. Street campaigns for freedom from the dictatorial Arab order continue as this book goes to press, in Bahrain, Yemen, Syria and beyond, many in the face of brutal suppression.

It's become known as the Arab Spring, but you'll also hear it referred to as the WikiLeaks revolution, because of information revealed in the US diplomatic cables about Tunisian corruption and – crucially – about US antipathy towards the country's president. Others briefly called it the Twitter revolution (or, in Egypt's case, the Facebook revolution), after the channels through which information about the protests spread, until they realised how disparaging this was to the people who were risking their lives to take to the streets and demand change.

Still, I couldn't help thinking back to what Julian had told me when I first met him, about how though free speech made very little difference to Western power structures, it could make all the difference in other parts of the world. It looks like he might have been on to something.

It turns out Rop was right, too, about the whiteboard with his name on it in Washington. Along with several other people who helped WikiLeaks release the *Collateral Murder* video in Reykjavik, he is currently fighting demands from the US Department of Justice for Twitter to hand over his communications records from that period.

But one thing Rop didn't have to worry about was his keynote address at 27c3 – that went down very well. Here's how he closed it:

> As we enter uncharted terrain, we are the first generation in a long time to see our leaders in a state of more or less complete helplessness. Most of today's politicians realize that nobody in their ministry or any of their expensive consultants can tell them what is going on anymore. They have a steering wheel in their hands without a clue what – if anything – it is connected to. Meanwhile the brakes are all worn out and the windy road at the bottom of the hill approaches. Politics is becoming more and more the act of looking at least slightly relaxed while silently praying the accident will happen sometime after your term is up.
>
> Now this all sounds really smug. Like we, the hackers, the geeks, somehow have all the answers. We don't. But we do have some important parts.
>
> For one we understand the extent to which complexity can be our enemy. We've optimized our privatized world to get that last 2% profitability. And we're already in a situation where everything we need comes just-in-time from China, assuming that we'll need exactly the same things today as we needed this time last year. Everything is interconnected and if one thing fails the whole system goes down. The winter chaos that has

broken out all over northern Europe is just another sign of this lack of slack.

We also live in a world that increasingly has different pockets of reality, different narratives. In that context, I think we can all see that our narrative is gaining importance.

At the same time Apple, Google, Facebook and the more geographically challenged traditional governments will try to make all of humanity enter their remaining secrets, they'll further lock us out of our own hardware and they'll eventually attempt to kill privacy and anonymity altogether.

We still have to tell most of the people out there, that privacy is not in fact brought about by some magic combination on the intentionally confusing privacy radiobutton page on Facebook. It does come from, among other things, code some of us have already written and code that we still need to write: we need many things by yesterday. And we need to properly security-audit the tools we build, even if that means we can't put in new features as quickly.

As for the future: it's going to be a mess. But I calmed down a lot when I decided for myself that this is not only bad news. Let's face it: the current situation was never sustainable anyway. And people, both in rich and in poor countries, are not very happy now. Just remember the massive loads of anti-depressants apparently needed to keep us going. The decline of the Roman Empire was probably a very interesting period to live in and for most inhabitants life simply went on, with or without Rome.

OK, so the world is going to be a mess for a bit... You are maybe asking yourself: "What do I do with this knowledge?" First of all, Jon Stewart nailed it when he recently said "we live in difficult times, not end times." The future is not about finding solitude and a farm on a hill, it's not about guns and ammo. But it is about having working trust relationships with the most varied group of people you can find. And it is about imagining beyond today and picking up a wide range of skills. It's about positioning yourself such that you have some flexibility. Even if everything stays the same, there's not much risk in any of that.

If on the other hand some of the structures around us indeed implode, we as a community will become no less important. Again: the world is not going to end. I promise there will be no zombies and humanity will survive. A lot of structures will survive. It's just going to be quite messy for a little bit.

If the shit hits the fan, a lot of things are going to be decentralized, but in a still very networked world. Some of us will likely be reverse engineering and then re-engineering systems to get rid of some of the crazy complexity and dependencies. Improvising and doing more with less is something we are good at, not to mention making things when we need them and repairing them instead of throwing them away.

We come in peace. We're not called Chaos Computer Club because we cause chaos. If anything, a lot of our collective work has actually prevented chaos by pointing out that maybe we should lay some decent virtual foundations before we build any more virtual skyscrapers.

Wau Holland explained the name to me: he felt there was universal validity in a set of – then rather new – theories that explained complex systems and behaviour from random events and very few very simple rules. This helped him explain a lot of how the world worked and how one could navigate the future.

We may not cause chaos, but we do understand some small part of how chaos works, and we have been able to help others deal with it better.

As this world becomes more chaotic and ad hoc, we can help.

Acknowledgements

From the beginning of this project, Rop Gonggrijp has offered me his time, advice and encouragement without ever losing patience or letting his own sizeable preoccupations distract him. I would like to offer him my warmest wishes and heartfelt thanks. I would like to thank all the people who have appeared in this book, and especially Ethan, Cory, Phil, Julian and Daniel. I'd also like to thank Frances Owen at Atlantic Books for her help securing my interview with Stewart Brand, and Mr Brand himself for his time and wisdom. Thanks also to Constanze Kurz of the Chaos Computer Club for helping me find my way around the Congress.

This book has been "flash published" outside of the traditional publishing world, and as such the only reason you are able to read it is thanks to the amazing work of an impromptu team of people who for reasons still mysterious to me volunteered their time and enthusiasm to make *Barefoot* happen. They are: Felix

Cohen, "the publishing geek", who was responsible for typesetting, e-publishing and charming the printers; Christopher Scally, "the artist", who was responsible for conceiving and executing the fantastic adaptations of John Tenniel's *Alice* drawings which illustrate this book; Kathryn Corrick, marketing guru and running mate; and Damien Morris, "the editor", who has the nicest way of letting you know when you're not making sense, and who re-inserted the hyphens, reminded me not everyone knows what "fuzzing" means and generally made the weeks running up to Felix's copy deadline a lot more pleasant that they rightfully should have been. Also thanks to my "beta testers", who read and commented on early drafts: John Hinton; Bill Thompson; Rufus Pollock; Cory Doctorow; Virginia Hogge; Polly Rossdale; Miranda Hinkley, Jamie Hall and Michael Holloway. Thanks guys – you all rock. Thanks too to David Bond and Ashley Jones of Green Lion Films for the advice, the enthusiasm – and the noodles.

I would never have had the courage to flash publish if it hadn't been for the encouraging words of several kind folk in the publishing world: Terence Blacker; Simon Prosser; Karolina Sutton; David Miller and Rupert Lancaster. Thanks also to Peter Law for his introduction to the world of book hacking and for his encouragement throughout.

I feel privileged to have been inspired, encouraged, entertained and nurtured by a wide variety of wonderful people whom I have no intention of naming here lest anyone suspect *Barefoot* is my one and only book. But I would like to extend a special thank you to James Casbon, my inspiration and in house tech support, for his faith, forgiveness and occasional good humour.

This book was typeset using Fanwell, an open source font freely available from the League of Moveable Type (http://www.theleagueofmoveabletype.com/), with titles set in Courier New, the iconic console font. Felix is indebted to the work put into assorted tools which allowed him to transform my final draft into the various electronic and paper formats in which this book now appears, all from the comfort of the command line. Props to James for the Perl scripts.

The illustrations which accompany this text have been adapted from drawings made by *Punch* cartoonist Sir John Tenniel to accompany the original editions of Lewis Carroll's books *Alice's Adventures in Wonderland* and *Alice Through the Looking Glass.* These drawings entered the public domain, meaning they could be reused and reinterpreted without seeking the original copyright holder's permission, on 1 January 1985, the year after the 70th anniversary of Tenniel's death in 1914. Which is good, because it would feel weird thanking a knight of the realm who was born 150 years before you were at the end of a book like this. Not that I'm not grateful or anything.

According to the Wikipedia entry *Works based on Alice in Wonderland*:

> *Alice's Adventures in Wonderland* and *Through the Looking-Glass* have been highly popular in their original forms, and have served as the basis for many subsequent works since they were published. They have been adapted directly into other media, their characters and situ-

ations have been appropriated into other works, and these elements have been referenced innumerable times as familiar elements of shared culture. Simple references to the two books are too numerous to list.

Glossary

The word "hacker" is used by different people to mean different things. In this book, I use it to mean mostly "computer enthusiast or hobbyist" and "person who likes taking things apart and seeing how they work". I do not use it in the sense that emerged in the mainstream media in the early nineties and persists to this day, namely "computer criminal" or perhaps "malicious and potentially maladjusted computer expert who likes using computers to hurt people and property" despite the fact that, as stated in the Wikipedia entry for *Hacker* "this usage has become so predominant that the general public is unaware that different meanings exist". Hopefully, now you've read this book, that statement no longer applies to you.

Within some of the communities this book has described, my use of the word hacker to mean both someone who builds software and tools and someone who tests the security of computer systems would not be uncontroversial. Some people like to call that last set of activities cracking, not hacking, and I've used "cracking" once or twice myself. Not all hacking is done with good intentions, of course. But thankfully for all of us, hackers have deployed a failsafe system for recognising each other's intentions, based on the wearing of hats. A white-hatted hacker works for the public good. A black-hatted hacker is motivated by malice or personal gain. A grey-hatted hacker is somewhere in between. Watch out for hackers wearing hats!

It's surprising how many people still don't understand the difference between the terms "internet" and "world wide web". John Humphreys, who presents Radio 4's flagship current affairs programme, *Today*, had to have it explained to him live on air earlier this year (although, come to think of it, that's not all that surprising). Put simply, the internet is a network of computers, or, more precisely, a network of networks of computers, and the web is one of several information resources served over that network (another one is email).

Some readers may find the following glossary helpful. Many of its entries are adapted from Wikipedia and to comply with Wikipedia's licensing terms, a digital copy of this glossary licensed under CC-BY-SA and with detailed attribution information is available at the following stable url: http://www.barefootintocyberspace.com/glossary.

26C3:
: 26th Chaos Communications Congress, held in Berlin in December 2009

27C3:
: 27th Chaos Communications Congress, held in Berlin in December 2010

ALTERNATIVE REALITY GAME:
: An interactive narrative game that uses the real world as its platform

APACHE:
: Web server software notable for playing a key role in the initial growth of the World Wide Web

BIT:
: The basic unit of information storage

BITTORRENT:
: A peer-to-peer communications protocol

BLACK BOX:
: A device or system which can be viewed solely in terms of its input and output, without any knowledge of its internal workings

BOTNET:
: A collection of infected computers ("bots") that have been taken over by crackers to perform malicious tasks or functions.

BULLETIN BOARD SYSTEMS (BBS):
: A precursor to the modern form of the World Wide Web, a system that allowed users to dial in to a central computer over a phone line using a modem in order to read news bulletins and swap messages with other users

CACHE:
: A software component that stores data so that future requests for that data can be served faster

c-Base:
: Berlin hackspace and nightclub

CCC:
: Chaos Computer Club *or* Chaos Communications Congress

CHIPPING :
: Installing a small electronic device used to modify or disable built-in restrictions and limitations of computers

CLONING:
: In the context of phones, transferring the identity of one mobile to another

CLOUD COMPUTING:
: Computational resources accessible via a computer network rather than from a local computer

COPYLEFT:
: A play on the word 'copyright' used to describe the practice of using copyright law to offer the right to distribute copies and modified versions of a work

CRC:
: Censorship Research Center

CRYPTOGRAPHY:
: The practice and study of hiding information

CULTURE-JAMMING:
: A tactic used by many anti-consumerist social movements to disrupt or subvert mainstream cultural institutions, including corporate advertising

CYBERPUNK:
: A postmodern and science fiction genre noted for its focus on high tech and low life

DARPA:
The Defense Advanced Research Projects Agency, an agency of the United States Department of Defense

DATA-MINING:
The process of extracting patterns from large data sets by combining methods from statistics and artificial intelligence with database management

DoS / DDoS:
A denial-of-service attack (DoS attack) or distributed denial-of-service attack (DDoS attack) is an attempt to make a computer resource unavailable to its intended users, usually by flooding it with traffic or requests.

EFF:
See Electronic Frontier Foundation

ELECTRONIC FRONTIER FOUNDATION:
US-based organisation that works to preserve digital rights and freedoms

FIRMWARE:
Fixed, small programs and/or data structures that internally control an electronic device

FLAME WAR:
A hostile and insulting interaction between internet users

FLASH MOB:
A group of people who assemble suddenly in a public place, perform an unusual and sometimes seemingly pointless act for a brief time, then disperse, often for the purposes of entertainment and/or satire.

FREE SOFTWARE:
Software that can be used, studied, and modified without restriction, and which can be copied and redistributed in modified or unmodified form either without restriction, or with restrictions that only ensure that further recipients can also do these things

FUZZING:
: Providing invalid, unexpected, or random data to the inputs of a computer program. The program is then monitored for exceptions such as crashes.

GNU:
: GNU's Not Unix (GNU), a recursive acronym

GNU/LINUX:
: A computer operating system also known as Linux. The development of GNU/Linux is one of the most prominent examples of free and open source software collaboration.

GSM:
: GSM (Global System for Mobile Communications), is a set of standards which describe technologies for second generation digitalcellular networks.

HOSTING / WEB HOSTS:
: Web hosts are companies that provide space on a server they own or lease for use by their clients as well as providing internet connectivity, typically in a data centre.

HYPERTEXT:
: Hypertext is text displayed on a computer or other electronic device with references (hyperlinks) to other text that the reader can immediately access, usually by a mouse click.

IM:
: Instant Message

ISP:
: Internet Service Provider

LA QUADRATURE DU NET:
: France-based organisation that works to preserve digital rights and freedoms

Mailman:
: A computer software application for managing electronic mailing lists

MAME:
: MAME (an acronym of Multiple Arcade Machine Emulator) is an emulator application designed to recreate the hardware of arcade game systems in software on modern personal computers and other platforms.

man-in-the-middle:
: A form of active eavesdropping in which the attacker makes independent connections with the victims and relays messages between them, making them believe that they are talking directly to each other over a private connection, when in fact the entire conversation is controlled by the attacker.

MIT:
: Massachusetts Institute of Technology

noobie:
: Hacker jargon for "newbie"

NORAD:
: North American Aerospace Defense Command

ONI:
: Open Net Initiative

Open Rights Group (ORG):
: UK-based organisation that works to preserve digital rights and freedoms

open source:
: Practices in production and development that promote access to the end product's source materials

ORG:
: *See* Open Rights Group

PAYWALL:

A paywall blocks access to a webpage with a screen requiring payment.

PDP11:

16-bit minicomputer sold by Digital Equipment Corporation (DEC) from 1970 into the 1990s

PEER-TO-PEER:

A distributed application architecture that partitions tasks or workloads between equally privileged participants in the application which are said to form a peer-to-peer network of nodes. The peer-to-peer application structure was popularised by file sharing systems like Napster.

PHREAKING:

A slang term coined to describe the activity of a culture of people who study, experiment with, or explore telecommunication systems, such as equipment and systems connected to public telephone networks.

PROTOCOL:

A communications protocol is a formal description of digital message formats and the rules for exchanging those messages in or between computing systems and in telecommunications.

RAINBOW TABLES:

A pre-computed table for reversing cryptographic hash functions, usually for cracking password hashes

ROUTER:

A device that forwards data packets across computer networks

SERVER / WEB SERVER / MAIL SERVER:

Web server can refer to either the hardware (the computer) or the software (the computer application) that helps to deliver content that can be accessed through the internet. A mail server runs software that transfers electronic mail messages from one computer to another.

SNIFFING:

Using a computer program or a piece of computer hardware that can intercept and log traffic passing over a digital network

SPOOFING:

In the context of network security, a spoofing attack is a situation in which one person or program successfully masquerades as another by falsifying data and thereby gaining an illegitimate advantage.

SRSLY?:

Hacker shorthand for "seriously?"

STEGANOGRAPHY:

The art and science of writing hidden messages in such a way that no one, apart from the sender and intended recipient, suspects the existence of the message

TCP/IP:

A set of communications protocols used for the internet and other similar networks.

TED:

Technology, Education Design - a series of international conferences

USENET:

A worldwide distributed internet discussion system

WALLED GARDEN:

A closed or exclusive set of information services

References

Assange, Julian, and Daniel Schmitt. 2009. WikiLeaks Release 1.0 presented at the 26th Chaos Communication Congress, December 27, Berlin. http://www.youtube.com/watch?v=8zNFe1mQ6Tc.

Ben Gharbia, Sami. 2010. The Internet Freedom Fallacy and the Arab Digital activism. September 17. http://samibengharbia.com/2010/09/17/the-internet-freedom-fallacy-and-the-arab-digital-activism/.

Blair, Tony. 2002. Prime Minister's keynote speech presented at the International e-Summit, November 19, London. http://webarchive.nationalarchives.gov.uk/20090101050155/number10.gov.uk/page1734.

Bogdanor, Vernon. 2006. "The rise and fall of the political party." *New Statesman*, October 23. http://www.newstatesman.com/200610230057.

Brand, Stewart (ed). Fall 1968. *Whole Earth Catalog.*

Brand, Stewart. 1972. "Space War: Fanatic Life and Symbolic Death Among the Computer Bums." *Rolling Stone*, December 7. http://www.wheels.org/spacewar/stone/rolling_stone.html.

——. 1974. "History - Demise Party etc." *Whole Earth Catalog*, October. http://wholeearth.com/issue/1180/article/321/history.-.demise.party.etc.

——. 1985. "Keep Designing: How the Information Economy is Being Created and Shaped by the Hacker Ethic." *Whole Earth Review*, May.

Brandeis, Louis. 1913. "What Publicity Can Do." *Harpers Weekly*.

Burns, John F. 2010. "WikiLeaks Founder on the Run, Trailed by Notoriety." *The New York Times*, October 23. http://www.nytimes.com/2010/10/24/world/24assange.html.

Bush, Vannevar. 1945. "As We May Think." *The Atlantic*, July. http://www.theatlantic.com/magazine/archive/1945/07/as-we-may-think/3881/.

Clay, Jason. 2010. How big brands can help save biodiversity presented at the TED Global, July, Oxford. http://www.ted.com/talks/jason_clay_how_big_brands_can_save_biodiversity.html.

Clinton, Hilary. 2010. Remarks on Internet Freedom Washington DC. http://www.state.gov/secretary/rm/2010/01/135519.htm.

Coghlan, Tom, and Giles Whittell. 2010. "Afghan informants' lives at risk from documents posted on WikiLeaks." *The Australian Times*, July 28. http://www.theaustralian.com.au/news/world/afghan-informants-lives-at-risk-from-documents-posted-on-wikileaks/story-e6frg6so-1225897924552.

Coupland, Douglas. 1991. *Generation X: Tales for an Accelerated Culture*. Canada: St Martin's Press.

dajmeister. 2010. *Cory Doctorow at the Protest against the Digital Economy Bill*. March 24. http://www.youtube.com/watch?v=ILwnY1RqS64.

Davies, Nick. 2009. *Flat Earth News: An Award-winning Reporter Exposes Falsehood, Distortion and Propaganda in the Global Media*. Great Britain: Vintage.

Deibert, Ronald, John Palfrey, Rafal Rohozinski, Jonathan Zittrain (eds.). 2008. *Access Denied: The Practice and Policy of Global Internet Filtering*. Cambridge: MIT Press.

Deibert, Ronald, John G. Palfrey, Rafal Rohozinski and Jonathan Zittrain (eds.). 2010. *Access Controlled: The Shaping of Power, Rights, and Rule in Cyberspace*. Cambridge: MIT Press.

Dobson, William J. 2010. "Needles in Haystack." *Newsweek*, August 6. http://www.newsweek.com/2010/08/06/needles-in-a-haystack.html#.

Doctorow, Cory. 2008. *Little Brother*. USA: Tor Teen.

Elmer-Dewitt, Philip, David S. Jackson, and Wendy King. 1993. "First Nation in Cyberspace." *Time*, December 6. http://www.time.com/time/magazine/article/0,9171,979768-1,00.html.

Engelbart, Douglas. 1968. The Mother of All Demos presented at the Fall Joint Computer Conference, December 6, San Francisco. http://sloan.stanford.edu/MouseSite/1968Demo.html.

Florin, Fabrice. 1984. Hackers: Wizards of the Electronic Age. United States. http://www.youtube.com/watch?v=bl_1OybdteY.

Garreau, Joel. 1994. "Conspiracy of Heretics." *Wired*, November. http://www.wired.com/wired/archive/2.11/gbn.html.

Gates, William Henry III. 1976. An Open Letter to Hobbyists. February 3. http://www.blinkenlights.com/classiccmp/gateswhine.html.

Gonggrijp, Rop. 2010. We Come In Peace presented at the 27th Chaos Communication Congress, December 27, Berlin. http://www.youtube.com/watch?v=7ZmtCUrx9to.

Gonggrijp, Rop, and Frank Rieger. 2005. We Lost The War presented at the 22nd Chaos Communication Congress, December 27, Berlin. http://video.google.com/videoplay?docid=-3755503618571546547#.

Grossman, Wendy. 1997. *net.wars*. United States: NYU Press.

Hopper, Dennis. 1969. *Easy Rider*.

Horvath, Michael D. 2008. *Wikileaks.org—An Online Reference to Foreign Intelligence Services, Insurgents, or Terrorist Groups?* Counterintelligence Analysis Report. US Department of Defense Intelligence Analysis Program (DIAP), March 18. http://wikileaks.org/file/us-intel-wikileaks.pdf.

Huxley, Aldous. 2004. *The Doors of Perception.* Great Britain: Vintage.

Jobs, Steve. 2005. 2005 Commencement Address June 12, Stanford. http://www.roj.com.np/life-inspiration/steve-jobs-how-to-live-before-you-die/.

Khatchadourian, Raffi. 2010. "No Secrets." *The New Yorker*, June 7. http://www.newyorker.com/reporting/2010/06/07/100607fa_fact_khatchadourian.

Klein, Naomi. 2000. *No Logo*. Flamingo.

Knight Lightning. 1989. "German Hackers Break Into Los Alamos and NASA", *Phrack,* March 29 http://www.phrack.org/issues.html?issue=25&id=10#article

Levine, Adam. 2010. "Top military official: WikiLeaks founder may have 'blood' on his hands." *cnn.com*, July 29. http://articles.cnn.com/2010-07-29/us/wikileaks.mullen.gates_1_julian-assange-leak-defense-robert-gates?_s=PM:US.

Levy, Steven. 1984. *Hackers: Heroes of the Computer Revolution.* Anchor Press / Doubleday.

———. 1994. *Insanely Great: The Life and Times of Macintosh, the Computer That Changed Everything.* Penguin.

Markoff, John. 2006. *What the Dormouse Said: How the Sixties Counterculture Shaped the Personal Computer Industry.* Great Britain: Penguin Books.

Marshall, John. 2009. *Membership of UK Political Parties.* Standard Note. London: House of Commons Library, August 17. http://www.parliament.uk/documents/commons/lib/research/briefings/snsg-05125.pdf.

Morozov, Evgeny. 2010a. Hay-what? *Net Effect.* September 2. http://neteffect.foreignpolicy.com/posts/2010/09/02/hay_what.

——. 2010b. On the irresponsibility of Internet intellectuals. *Net Effect.* October 13. http://neteffect.foreignpolicy.com/posts/2010/09/13/on_the_irresponsibility_of_internet_intellectuals.

Morris, John G. Pictures of war and protest. http://frontline.rocksolidsolutions-uk.com/words-and-pictures/photography/.

Murdoch, Rupert. 2009. Rupert Murdoch Before the Federal Trade Commission's Workshop: From Town Crier to Bloggers: How Will Journalism Survive the Internet Age?, December 1, Washington DC. http://www.newscorp.com/news/news_435.html.

O'Brien, Danny. 2010. Haystack vs How The Internet Works. *Oblomovka.* September 14. http://www.oblomovka.com/wp/2010/09/14/haystack-vs-how-the-internet-works/.

Perry Barlow, John. 1990. "Crime and Puzzlement", June 8. http://w2.eff.org/Misc/Publications/John_Perry_Barlow/HTML/crime_and_puzzlement_1.html.

———. 1996. A Declaration of the Independence of Cyberspace. February 8. https://projects.eff.org/~barlow/Declaration-Final.html.

PlentyMag.com. 2009. "The Whole Earth Catalog Effect." *PLENTY Magazine*, May 19. http://www.mnn.com/lifestyle/arts-culture/stories/the-whole-earth-catalog-effect?page=1.

Poulsen, Kevin, and Kim Zetter. 2010. U.S. Intelligence Analyst Arrested in Wikileaks Video Probe. *Threat Level*. June 6. http://www.wired.com/threatlevel/2010/06/leak/.

Roush, Wade. 2009. "Arbor Networks Reports on the Rise of the Internet 'Hyper Giants'." *Xconomy*, October 20. http://www.xconomy.com/boston/2009/10/20/arbor-networks-reports-on-the-rise-of-the-internet-hyper-giants/.

Schneier, Bruce. 2000. *Secrets and Lies: Digital Security in a Networked World*. United States: John Wiley & Sons.

Stone, C.J. 1996. *Fierce Dancing: Adventures in the Underground*. Faber and Faber.

The Economist. 2007. "TED: Davos for Optimists." *The Economist*, March 8. http://www.economist.com/blogs/freeexchange/2007/03/ted_davos_for_optimists.

The Guardian. 2010a. "Afghanistan: The War Logs." *The Guardian*, July 25. http://www.guardian.co.uk/world/the-war-logs.

———. 2010b. "Iraq: The War Logs." *The Guardian*, October 22. http://www.guardian.co.uk/world/iraq-war-logs.

———. 2010c. "The US embassy cables." *The Guardian*, November 29. http://www.guardian.co.uk/world/the-us-embassy-cables.

The Washington Post. 2010. "Top Secret America." *Washington Post*, September 17. http://projects.washingtonpost.com/top-secret-america.

Thiessen, Marc. 2010. "WikiLeaks must be stopped." *Washington Post*, August 3. http://www.washingtonpost.com/wp-dyn/content/article/2010/08/02/AR2010080202627.html.

Turner, Fred. 2006. *From Counterculture to Cyberculture: Stewart Brand, the Whole Earth Network, and the Rise of Digital Utopianism*. United States: The University of Chicago Press.

WikiLeaks. 2010. *Collateral Murder*. April 5. http://www.collateralmurder.com/.

Wolfe, Tom. 1989. *The Electric Kool-Aid Acid Test*. Great Britan: Black Swan.

York, Jillian. 2010. *Policing Content in the Quasi-Public Sphere*. Bulletin. September 21. http://opennet.net/policing-content-quasi-public-sphere.

Zemeckis, Robert. 1985. *Back to the Future*.

Zuckerman, Ethan. New Berkman Paper on DDoS – silencing speech is easy, protecting it is hard. *My Heart's in Accra*. http://www.ethanzuckerman.com/blog/2010/12/20/new-berkman-paper-on-ddos-silencing-speech-is-easy-protecting-it-is-hard/.

Zuckerman, Ethan, Hal Roberts, Ryan McGrady, Jillian York, and John Palfrey. 2010. *2010 Report on Distributed Denial of Service (DDoS) Attacks*. Berkman Center for Internet and Society, December 20. http://cyber.law.harvard.edu/publications/2010/DDoS_Independent_Media_Human_Rights.

Index

Lightning Source UK Ltd.
Milton Keynes UK
UKOW020559280911

179419UK00003B/1/P